MAKING & DECORATING

FANTASTIC FRAMES

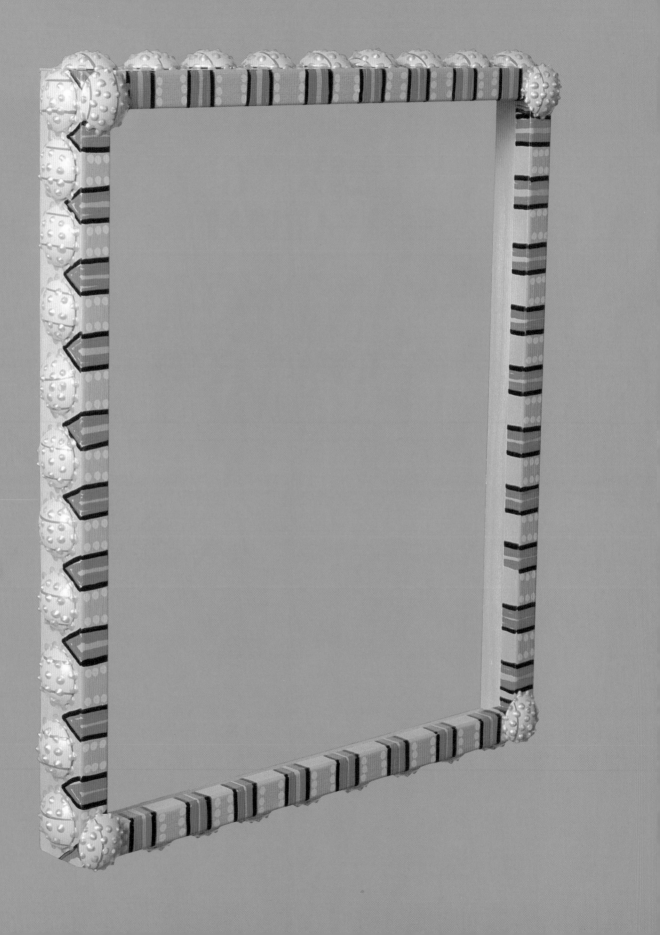

MAKING & DECORATING

FANTASTIC FRAMES

*More than 100
Unusual Techniques
& Projects*

Thom Boswell

A Sterling/Lark Book

Sterling Publishing Co., Inc.   New York

Design: Chris Colando
Production: Elaine Thompson, Chris Colando
Photography: Evan Bracken

Library of Congress Cataloging-in-Publication Data
Boswell, Thom.
    Making and decorating fantastic frames : more than 100 unusual
techniques and projects / by Thom Boswell.
        p.   cm.
    "A Sterling/Lark book."
    Includes index.
    ISBN 0-8069-0287-6
    1. Picture frames and framing.   I. Title.
    N8550.B69   1993
    749'.7--dc20   92-39104
                                                          CIP

10 9 8 7 6 5 4 3 2 1

A Sterling/Lark Book

First paperback edition published in 1994 by
Sterling Publishing Company, Inc.
    387 Park Avenue South, New York, N.Y. 10016

Produced and © 1993 by Altamont Press, Inc.
    50 College Street, Asheville, N.C.

Distributed in Canada by Sterling Publishing
    % Canadian Manda Group, P.O. Box 920, Station U
    Toronto, Ontario, Canada M8Z 5P9
Distributed in Great Britain and Europe by Cassell PLC
    Villiers House, 41/47 Strand, London WC2N 5JE, England
Distributed in Australia by Capricorn Link (Australia) Pty Ltd.
    P.O. Box 6651, Baulkham Hills, Business Centre, NSW 2153, Australia

Sterling ISBN 0-8069-0287-6 Trade
                0-8069-0288-4 Paper

CONTENTS

INTRODUCTION The New Art of Picture Framing 6

TRADITIONAL CONSTRUCTION TECHNIQUES
Creating Mouldings and Liners.......................8
Cutting and Joining Mouldings 10
Cutting Mats and Glass 12
Mounting and Assembling 14
Hanging and Other Formats.........................16

FRAMING PROJECTS
Revivals and Revamping................................18
Easy Enough for Kids 24
Milled Woods 30
Natural Woods 38
Shaped and Painted Woods..........................50
Special Finishes 58
Fabric Coverings 72
Woven Materials 80
Paper Treatments 86
Earthen Castings 94
Stained Glass 100
Motifs in Metal 106
Found Objects 114
Shadow Boxes 122
Mats and Liners 128

ARTIST'S DIRECTORY..................................143

SUGGESTED READING..................................144

METRIC EQUIVALENCY CHART 144

INDEX 144

INTRODUCTION
THE NEW ART OF PICTURE FRAMING

The common notion of a picture frame is a rectangle of mitered moulding. Even so-called custom framing seldom ventures beyond a traditionally accepted range of style and design. But what might framing look like if it was truly custom designed for the vast array of art being produced in this century?

A number of artists are beginning to answer that question. They are working in most every imaginable medium and sometimes producing frames that are works of art in their own right, suited only to framing mirrors. Of course, a frame should enhance rather than compete with its subject. Perhaps this creative exuberance demonstrates the latency of an art form too long ignored.

A picture frame is certainly more than a protective encasement, and it ought to be more than a stylistic formality used to legitimize every would-be work of art. In order to effectively complement its subject, a frame must be free to assume whatever size, shape, colors, materials and configurations the framer envisions. Long established principles of design may be called upon, but ultimately the framer explores and makes choices intuitively, and success or failure is recognized subjectively.

This book, like the playfully wrought frames displayed within, is an adventure. It utilizes proven techniques, but explores new approaches and encourages experimentation. It is a celebration of discovery and innovation, and therefore, always a beginning.

Besides this book, there are countless other sources of inspiration. But the most important one is the actual piece you wish to frame. Second to this is the aesthetic of the space in which it is displayed, yet this may change. Inspect the work of art (whether painting, photo, collage, etc.) for color, texture, theme, motif or any other design elements to be drawn upon. Meditate on the essence of the work and how it makes you feel. Respond imaginatively with a full palette of as many materials and techniques as you have at your command. (So many media are represented in this book that they cannot be fully explained in one volume, but the reading list will get you started.)

The challenge is to look at framing in new ways—to keep shifting your frame of reference. A frame can be both a border, defining the boundary of a subject, and a window, a portal that focuses and invites boundless perception. Construct a framework to shape, fit, arrange and enclose the spirit of your art. If you let the art become the frame, the frame will become art.

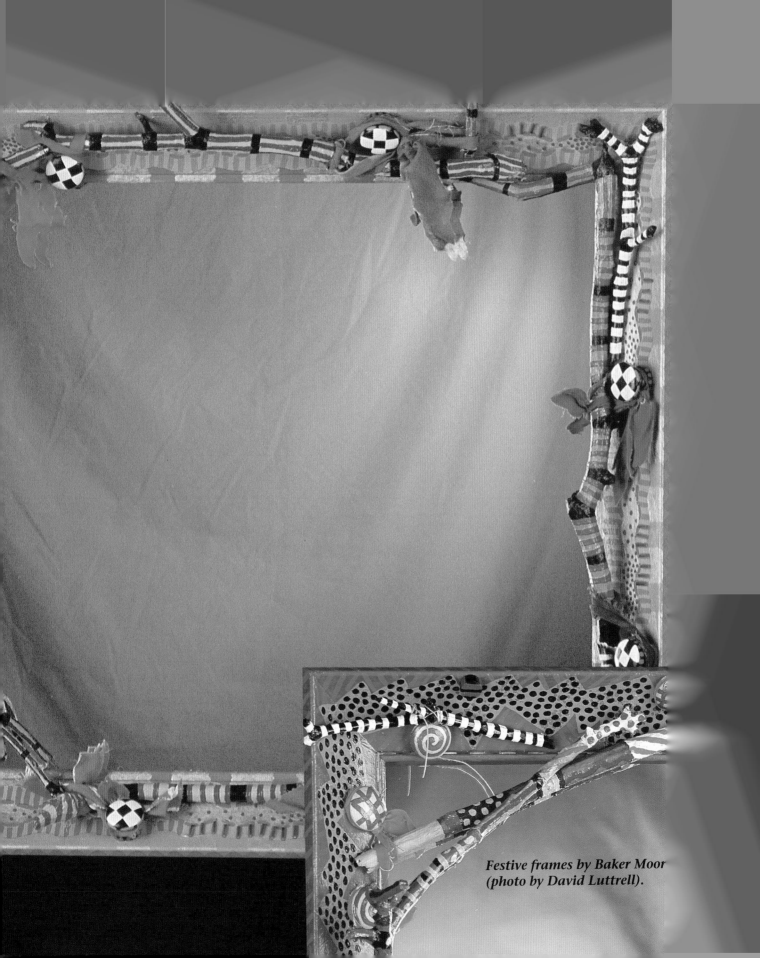

Festive frames by Baker Moor (photo by David Luttrell).

TRADITIONAL CONSTRUCTION TECHNIQUES

CREATING MOULDINGS & LINERS

If you have a table saw, you can shape a significant variety of mouldings. They can be rip cut from a single strip of wood, or assembled as a composite of several contoured strips glued and clamped together. If you have a router, your contouring capabilities will be multiplied. Even if you have neither of these tools, you can create an impressive range of mouldings by assembling composites of stock mouldings available at any lumber yard.

For many of the designs in this book, the foundation moulding is nothing more than a flat, wide strip, joined in a conventional mitered fashion. Many other foundations are cut from a single sheet of plywood, requiring only a standard hand saw or coping saw. In either case, the trick is to create a rabbet or lip which will hold the art assembly. If your wide, solid strip or plywood is thick enough (1/2" or more), you can rip cut a rabbet on your

Stock mouldings available from building suppliers

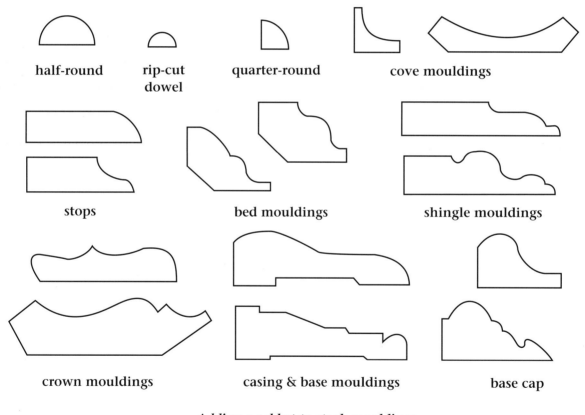

half-round   rip-cut dowel   quarter-round   cove mouldings

stops   bed mouldings   shingle mouldings

crown mouldings   casing & base mouldings   base cap

Adding a rabbet to stock mouldings

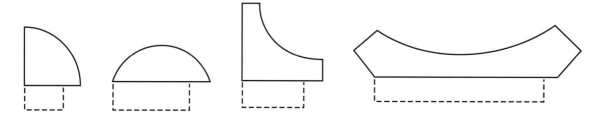

Mouldings cut on a table saw

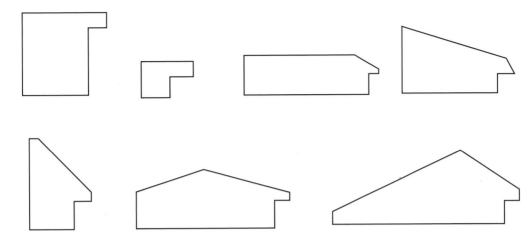

Composite mouldings using stock pieces and table saw

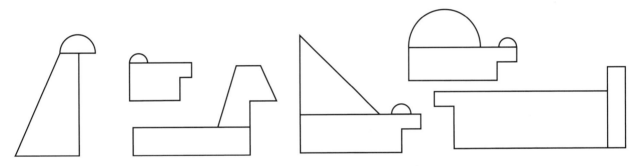

Composite mouldings using a router

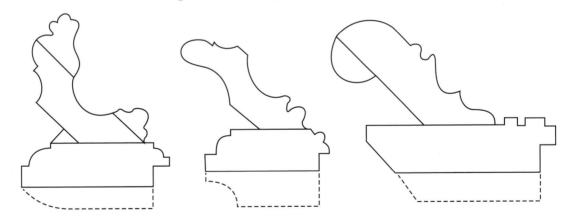

table saw. If not, add a rabbet by gluing and nailing strips around the back side of the window opening, recessed about 1/4". The strips should be at least 1/4" deep, and can either be custom cut or purchased as lattice. Oil paintings need a deeper rabbet.

Liners generally have a flat, wide face that is covered with fabric. They act as frames within frames and need to be measured accordingly. Rubber cement, white glue or library past should be sprayed or smeared on the face and around the rabbet. The fabric can be pressed on before or after the moulding is miter cut.

CUTTING AND JOINING MOULDINGS

Accurate measuring is crucial to successful framing. Since the art assembly will be fit into the recessed opening created by the rabbet, the dimensions of each side must be marked on the inside edge of the rabbet. Measure each side of the piece to be framed, then add 1/8" for a comfortable tolerance before cutting the moulding.

Professional framers usually use a sophisticated miter cutting tool called a chopper or guillotine. They will cut your moulding quite accurately for a price. Chances are, you'll do fine on your own with a conventional miter box, either purchased commercially or constructed at home (see Figure 1). The saw channels of your homemade box can be marked using a carpenter's square or a protractor. A radial arm saw would also suffice, provided you use a fine tooth blade.

The other most invaluable tool is an angle clamp. This enables accurate and efficient joining of 90° mitered corners. You may get by with a bench vise or improvise with C-clamps. There's even a tool consisting of four L-brackets with cinching line. In addition to a clamping system, you will need a drill (preferably electric), a small hammer and nail set.

Once you've cut your corners, wrap sandpaper around a block and gently sand any rough edges.

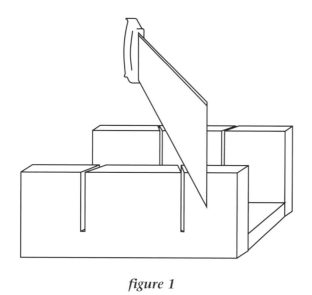

figure 1

figure 2

Be careful not to round the cut surface. Apply carpenter's glue evenly to the cut surfaces of two adjoining ends to form the first corner. There should be just enough glue to bulge around the seam when joined. Lay both sides into the angle clamp, tighten them very slightly back and forth until the corner is evenly joined. If the moulding is soft or has a delicate finish, pad the outer clamps with small strips of matboard to prevent denting the edge.

Using a small drill, prepare parallel holes for the nails at the corner through one side and into the endgrain of the other wherever it is thickest. Use small brads for small frames and larger finishing nails for larger frames. One nail in each corner of a miniature frame is sufficient, two nails for medium frames and three for large. Use a drill bit that is slightly smaller than the nail, or snip off the head of whatever nail you're using and drill with it. Tap the nails in gently (Fig. 2), then use a nail set to recess the heads. Wipe away any excess glue with a moist paper towel. The nail holes can be caulked with bits of putty or crayons that match the moulding, then rubbed smooth.

If using a bench vise, clamp the longer side of moulding before gluing. Stack some objects (e.g. wood scraps) to a height that will support the adjacent side of moulding wherever it will extend over the bench. Apply glue, then drill and nail the joint while holding the adjacent side with your other hand. It will rest on the stack of shims while drying. This method requires practice and a steady

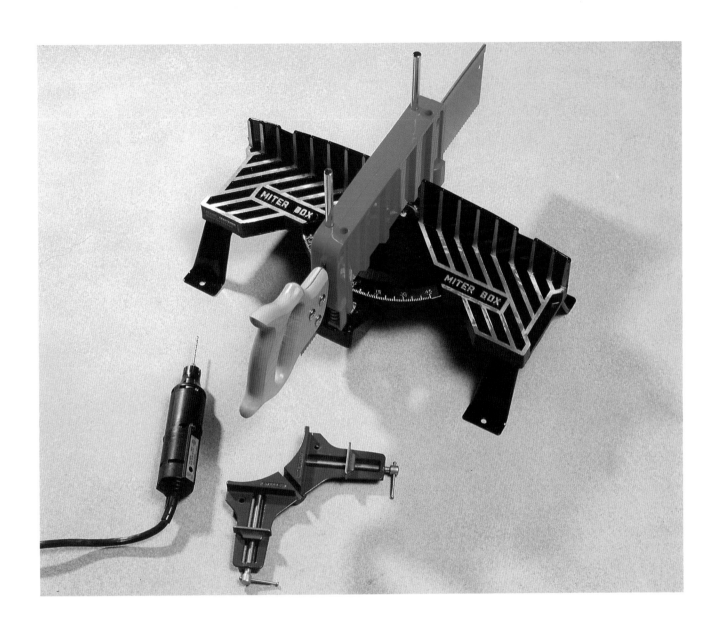

hand. C-clamps can be used to hold corners together on a flat work surface.

After joining the first corner, join the other two sides the same way and let dry. Next, apply glue to each remaining corner and clamp both L-shaped sections into place, forming a tight seam. Drill and nail this corner, then unclamp it, gently rotate the frame 180°, clamp and join the last corner. Shims may be needed to support the portion of the frame opposite the clamp so as not to pop the third corner before the glue has dried. This is especially critical when using a bench vise.

Frame Shape	No. Sides	Mitre Box Angle
Equilateral Triangle	3	60°
Pentagon	5	36°
Hexagon	6	30°
Octagon	8	22.5°
Decagon	10	18°
Dodecagon	12	15°

CUTTING MATS AND GLASS

Matboard is available in many colors and also varies slightly in thickness. If your artwork is particularly valuable, use acid-free rag board for both matting and backing.

Always work on a clean surface, since matboard blemishes easily. All marking and cutting should be done on the back side for the same reason. After you have cut the outer dimensions of the mat, mark the position of the window from each edge (see Figure 1). The convention on margins is to add a bit more space below the window. This compensates for the optical illusion of the window appearing lower than center when equal margins are used.

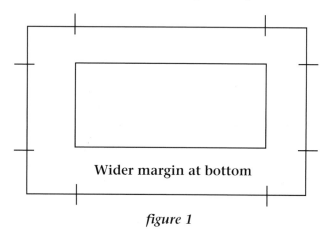

Wider margin at bottom

figure 1

Lay the mat face down on an old backing board that you don't mind scarring when the knife tip cuts past the mat. Lay a metal straight edge on the window side of one of the marked lines. A straight, perpendicular cut is easy to make, but isn't nearly as appealing as a bevel cut. Using a razor sharp mat knife, tilt the blade about 60° and adjust the straight edge until the blade hits the mark (see Fig. 2). Draw the blade down the line smoothly, main-

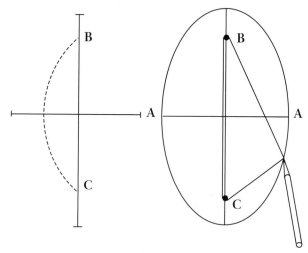

figure 3

taining a 60° tilt. The cut should extend 1/16" beyond the intersecting lines at each end to complete the corners. After cutting all four sides, the center should fall out. If it doesn't, carefully finish the corner cuts with a razor blade.

Oval windows are much more challenging, both to mark and cut. Mark the four center points of the height and width of the oval you want. Draw a cross between these points (see Fig. 3). Set a compass to half the length of the longer of the cross lines, then mark an arc from point A to determine points B and C. Tack nails firmly through B and C, then tie a loop of non-stretch string equal to the ABC triangle. Put a pencil inside the loop and draw the oval. Since cutting is most difficult, use thin matboard or card stock and don't attempt a bevel cut.

Rather than standard window glass, use the lighter weight picture glass. The technique used for cutting glass may seem a bit formidable to the novice, but can be mastered fairly easily with a little practice. You will need a glass cutter, a black felt-tip pen, a

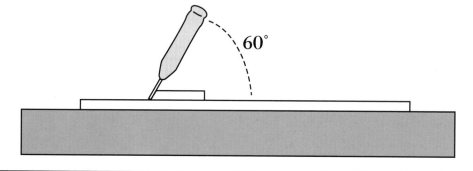

60°

figure 2

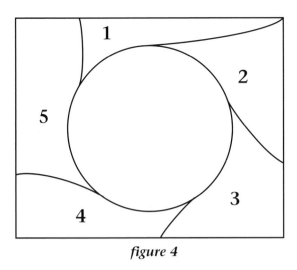

figure 4

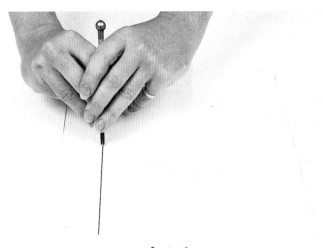

photo 1

straight edge ruler, and some glass scraps to practice a few cuts.

First, measure and draw the exact shape onto the glass with the pen and the ruler, with lines extending fully to all edges. Place the glass on a table in front of you. Hold the glass cutter with the fingertips of both hands, lay the wheel on the far end of one of your longer marks, and draw it straight toward you down the mark until it rolls off the near edge (see Photo 1). The motion should be smooth and continuous with moderate, even pressure. You must score the glass only once for each cut. Keeping the wheel of your cutter oiled will prolong its life.

photo 2

Once the glass is scored, grasp the near edge with thumbs over fists either side of the scored line, yet close together (see Photo2). Rotate fists firmly, with thumbs turning out from each other, pushing up from underneath to snap the glass apart and down the cut in one motion. If you are cutting stained glass, do not coax this process by first tapping under the scored cut with the ball end of the cutter. This creates uneven edges unsuitable for soldering stained glass joints. When cutting stained or textured glass, always score the smooth side. Also, be sure to wear safety goggles when cutting glass.

Cutting gentle curves utilizes this same technique. Severe and multiple curves are more difficult. To cut a circle, score and break a series of lines (as shown in Fig. 4), then even up the edge by chipping off irregularities with the notches in your glass cutter (see Photo 3).

photo 3

MOUNTING AND ASSEMBLING

Much of the art you wish to frame will need to be mounted in some fashion on to a board. You'll need a stiff board that won't warp with moisture and, if your art is valuable, one that's acid-free. Some of the varieties to consider are foam-core, upson board, heavy matboard, illustration board and chipboard.

You may want to topmount your art on a colored matboard, leaving a margin of board around it. Sometimes you'll cover this margin with a window mat that overlaps the edges of the art. At other times your art will fill the frame and be mounted to a board the same size. In this case, if the art is pressed to the glass with stiff backing board, no adhesive mounting may be necessary.

Wet mounting is complex, risky, and seldom used any more except for restoration. The most common method used nowadays is adhesive mounting. Spray rubber cement evenly over the back of the art, let dry until tacky, then press it to the board. Since you won't be able to reposition the art, cut the board after it is in place. There is also a double-backed adhesive film that can be used. The other major method is called dry mounting. This requires an adhesive coated mounting tissue that is activated by heat and pressure. A piece of tissue is cut to the size of the art, then tacked to the mounting board at two corners with a hot iron (set for "wool"). The art is positioned on the tissue and a sheet of paper over top. The iron is pressed over this, then again over the back side.

Valuable or delicate works of art should be mounted differently. Any materials that touch the art should be acid-free. The art should not touch the glass, and it should be attached to the mounting board with adhesive-backed linen tape at the top corners. Pastels and charcoal should also be separated from the glass with spacers (strips of mounting board or wood) around the perimeter. If you attach your art to a board with tape, do so only along the top edge to prevent buckling from moisture.

Once you have cut all the components to fit the frame, cleaned the glass and removed all dust and debris, it's time to assemble the piece. Add a stiff backing board for large frames or if you think the other components may warp over time. Stack all the layers, with glass on top, then run masking tape around the edges to seal the assembly. Be careful not to overlap the glass edge past the rabbet of the frame where it will show. (Taping is optional.)

Lay the frame, face down, on a clean work surface. Place the assembly inside the frame. It can be secured with a glazier's gun that fires points into the frame. Small brads also work nicely, and can be tapped in gently with a flat-sided hammer or pressed in with a flat metal object. In either case, the frame side that you're nailing should be butting up against something solid. If your work table lacks this, tack on a strip of wood to nail against or find some other area to work.

As a final step, seal the back of the assembly with heavy paper, such as brown paper grocery bags. Run a bead of white glue around the back edge of the frame. Lay the paper over this, press, then spray it generously with water. As the glue dries and the paper shrinks, trim the excess paper with a razor blade.

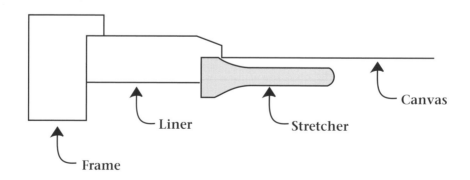

Frame   Liner   Stretcher   Canvas

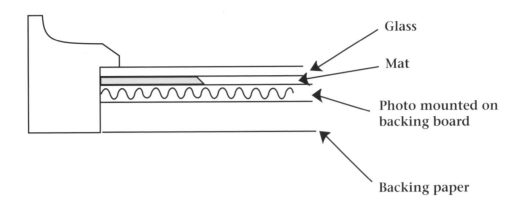

Glass

Mat

Photo mounted on
backing board

Backing paper

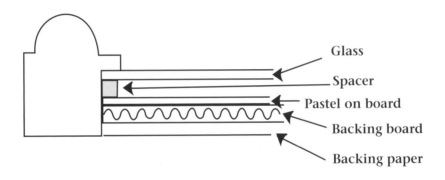

Glass

Spacer

Pastel on board

Backing board

Backing paper

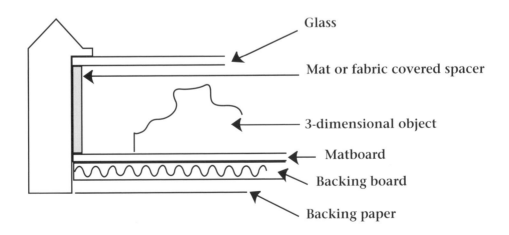

Glass

Mat or fabric covered spacer

3-dimensional object

Matboard

Backing board

Backing paper

HANGING AND OTHER FORMATS

Most pictures are displayed on a wall, and the most common hanging method involves two eyescrews and braided wire. These are available in different sizes and should be matched with the weight of the picture. Start the holes with an awl or a nail in the frame sides about one-third of the way down from the top. Be careful that the eyescrews don't protrude through the frame's face. Pass one end of some braided wire through one of the eyescrews about 3"–4", loop it through again, then wind it back around the main length of wire. Cut the wire to a sufficient length that you can tie off the other end the same way plus leave a little slack between the eyescrews.

In place of eyescrews you can use D rings (Figure 1). These will allow the picture to hang flat against the wall. For smaller pictures you can use a sawtooth hanger. These must be fastened at the center of gravity in order to work properly. The extra weight of large pictures can be supported with a loop of doubled wire through multiple eyescrews (Fig. 2). This counteracts the bowing tendency of the moulding by pulling it together. Metal wall hooks should be used instead of nails for all but the smallest of pictures.

You may occasionally want to convert a small stan-dard frame into a free-standing table frame. Cut a piece of plywood to fit into the back of the frame. This may be held in place with brads or swivel pins (as shown in Fig. 3). Cut a necktie shape from the plywood. You may simply attach it to the back with a metal hinge, or make a crankshaft-shape cut in the narrow end and drive brads through both sides to make your own hinge. A length of ribbon or chain can connect the back panel to the leg to keep it from falling open.

There are other ways of supporting small table frames. Easels can be constructed out of various materials to suit most any decor. The side of a frame may be fitted into a groove of some heavy object you have sculpted. A picture can be sand-wiched between two panes of plexiglass, then slipped inside grooves incorporated into any sort of stand you care to build.

An interesting alternative to standard wall mount-ing is the ledge. A narrow shelf, preferably with a groove or lip to hold the frame, can be fashioned decoratively using any of the techniques described in this book. They can support one or more frames as well as complementary knickknacks and a vase of flowers.

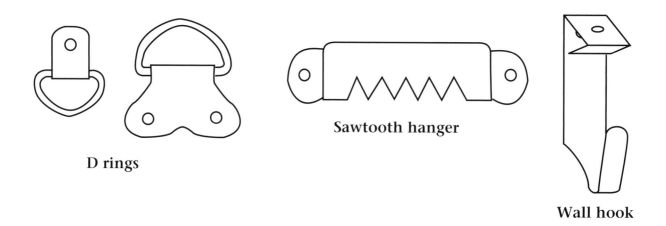

D rings

Sawtooth hanger

Wall hook

figure 1

TRADITIONAL CONSTRUCTION TECHNIQUES

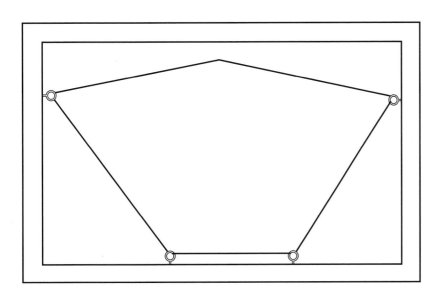

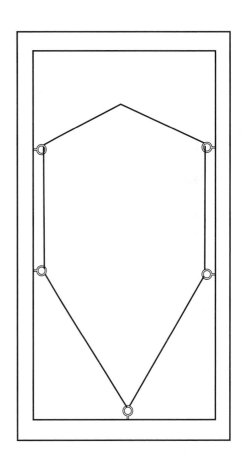

figure 2

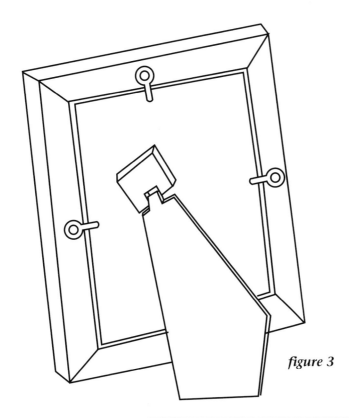

figure 3

REVIVALS & REVAMPING

Frames can eventually show their age in a number of ways. Nicks, chips and scratches accumulate, woods darken, metallic finishes lose their luster, and corners pop open. Yet old frames retain great appeal, especially old styles that are no longer being produced. Even the less interesting frames have value as a foundation for a new treatment. Old frames are relatively easy to revive in one way or another, and usually worth the effort.

Restoring a frame to its original condition can require specific methods too complex to explain in a book of this kind, but let's consider some general guidelines. If only one corner joint is cracked, loosen it just enough to squirt glue into the seam, clamp it, add a new nail and wipe away the excess glue. Large frames may need a steel L-bracket for reinforcement. Usually two or more corners will have popped. In this case, gently crack and disassemble the frame. (If you also plan to strip and refinish the moulding, now is the time.) Use a sandpaper block to remove all old glue and even up the seams. You can also cut new lengths if you wish. Rejoin the frame using slightly larger nails in the

old holes, or nail in new positions altogether.

Depending on the old finish, use a compatible stripping agent to remove it. Rags and/or fine steel wool are used. Interesting effects can be achieved with only partial removal of the old finish. If you strip all the way, the wood can either be stained, varnished, primed and painted, or gilded. Stains can be brushed on thick or rubbed to reveal the grain. A coat of sealer can be satin or glossy. A clear spar varnish will yellow nicely. If you plan to paint, nicks can be caulked beforehand. Gilding is less expensive with faux gold leaf (see chapter on Special Finishes). Spray paints provide another set of options.

Some old frames just beg for a little sprucing up, and can even serve as a point of departure for total revamping. Many of the imaginative treatments in this book use an old or otherwise uninteresting frame as a foundation. There's no limit to the number of materials and methods you can use to embellish any basic frame. You can choose your own style, and customize any frame to suit both the subject and the decor in which it will be displayed.

Because of the gesso relief and fluting on this frame, applying gold leaf would be quite tedious. An easier way to achieve a classic gold finish would be to simply paint on any one of the many gold paints commercially available. These can be applied either as a spray or with a brush.

The antique look for this frame was produced by brushing on gold paint that had been slightly thinned, then rubbing it down with a rag to expose the grain. Another antique effect can be achieved by applying a base coat of rusty red paint. After it has dried, apply a gold paint and gently rub it down to expose hints of the red undercoat.

Both of these frames utilize a conventional technique commonly referred to as "antiquing." The circular frame begins with a greenish base coat. The darker speckles can be spattered on or applied with a coarse sponge. Copper paint is then sponged onto the raised areas.

The rectangular frame has a base coat of off-white. Lavender is sponged on unevenly over this. The gold is sponged gently over the raised areas. Two applications of gold may be necessary.

As this frame illustrates, marbling need not be limited to flat surfaces. With one quick dip this old frame has undergone a unique revival. (For marbling techniques, see the Suggested Reading list.)

This old bureau mirror has been revamped into a picture frame with a series of scallop cuts and a new paint job. Because the latex primer and paint covers the wood grain, blemishes could be caulked and sanded.

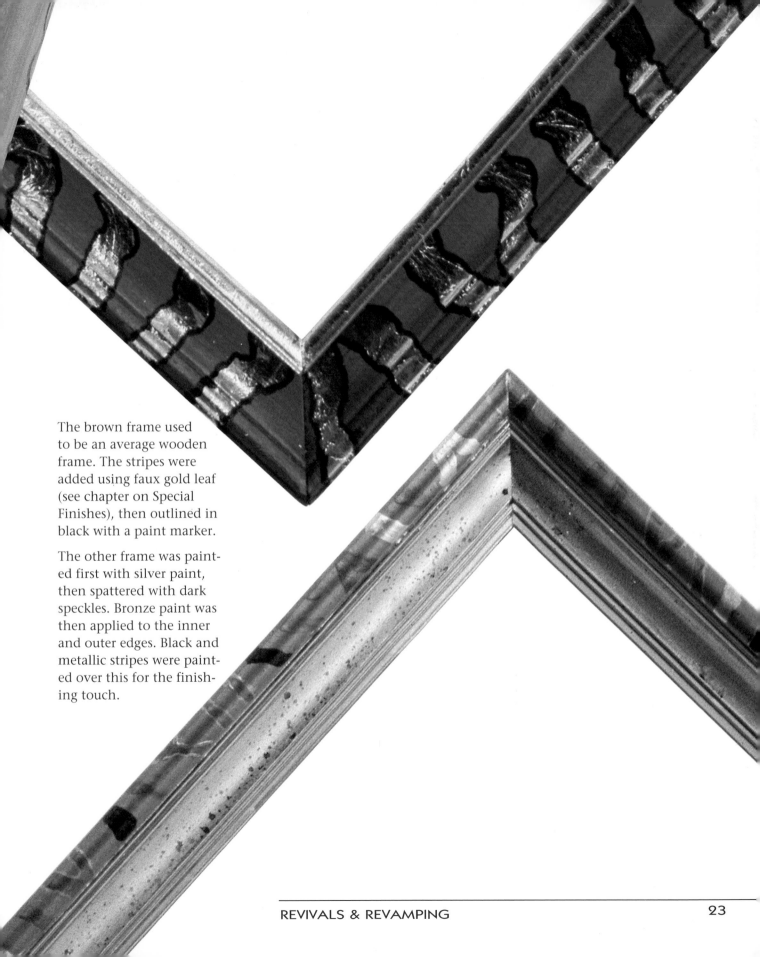

The brown frame used to be an average wooden frame. The stripes were added using faux gold leaf (see chapter on Special Finishes), then outlined in black with a paint marker.

The other frame was painted first with silver paint, then spattered with dark speckles. Bronze paint was then applied to the inner and outer edges. Black and metallic stripes were painted over this for the finishing touch.

EASY ENOUGH FOR KIDS

Children create a prolific amount of art, whether for relatives, school, their bedroom decoration or the ever available refrigerator. Because of the transitory nature of their art, framing possibilities are expanded.

Foundations need not last twenty years or more. Consequently, materials such as corrugated cardboard, matboard, foamcore, thin plywood, or inexpensive frames can be considered. These raw materials can be cut (by adults) from a single piece. Therefore joining is unnecessary, and creativity can be focused on decorative techniques.

Virtually every material available to children can be used to decorate any foundation. You might even consider providing a number of foundations and letting them rely on their own creativity to decorate them. A little supervision might improve the results, but consider the inspiration a child will find in the following tools: any kind of paints, felt-tip markers, finger paints, potato block prints, all sorts of decorative stickers, decorative tapes, unlimited comics and magazine cutouts. Open yourself to the possibilities. Your children might amaze you.

Your child sees an adorable picture of a duck in a magazine and can't resist clipping it out. Here's what to do when she insists on hanging it in her room. Let her tear out a few color pages of a newspaper. She can roll them diagonally into tubes and tape them closed. String is used to tie the tubes together and a loop for hanging. The picture is taped to the frame.

Spray a thick coat of faux granite paint on a black mat board. Scratch through the wet paint with any flat tool (spatula, screwdriver, fork, etc.) to create a pattern. Let dry, then spray with acrylic sealant.

Start with a 100% white cotton mat board. Cut a window. Place newspaper over the mat and iron it to heat the mat surface. Scribble with crayons around the inside edge of the mat. Scatter crayon shavings with a crayon sharpener all over the mat. Gently place newspaper over the mat and iron again.

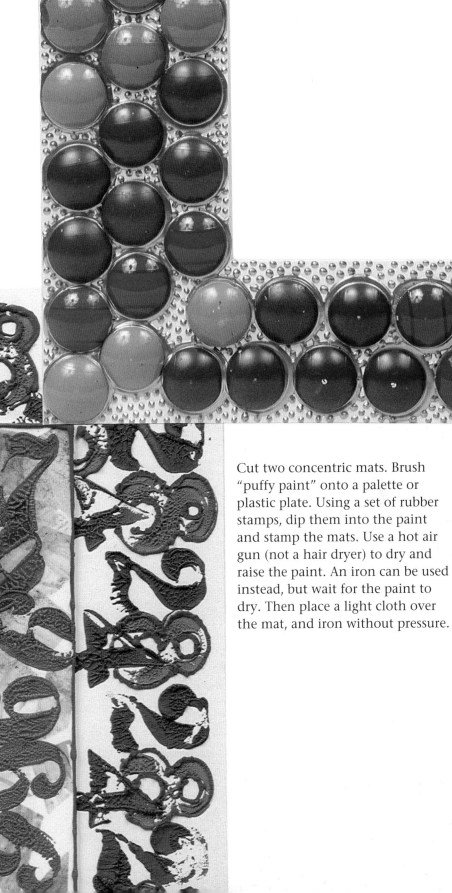

The rounded disks are plastic clip-on earring parts. They are painted, then glued to the mat board or foam-core. Glow dimensional paint is used to fill in the spaces with dots.

Cut two concentric mats. Brush "puffy paint" onto a palette or plastic plate. Using a set of rubber stamps, dip them into the paint and stamp the mats. Use a hot air gun (not a hair dryer) to dry and raise the paint. An iron can be used instead, but wait for the paint to dry. Then place a light cloth over the mat, and iron without pressure.

Invest in a few sets of children's stickers, or let them use up ones they've collected. For a high density collage, first attach scraps of the sticker material that surrounds the stickers. After filling the mat board with overlapping stickers, criss-cross them with colored tapes, such as metallic or cloth tapes or architectural tape.

Cut a colored mat or spray paint it. Let your child
clip out his favorite comics, then glue them to the
mat. They can be outlined with a colored marker.
If you have rubber stamps, he can stamp his
name or other words all around the comics.
Spray with clear acrylic sealant.

MILLED WOODS

If you have sufficient tools and resources, the possibilities for framing with wood are almost limitless. Power tools and commercially available milled woods allow you to execute a wonderful array of sophisticated designs. Even with a window cut out of a single piece of solid or plywood, you can add all sorts of design elements such as cutouts, inlay, silhouettes, drilled circles, carving or woodburning patterns.

Hybrid mouldings can be created by joining stock mouldings (see page 8), or by shaping and joining your own. Simply by cutting dado grooves on a table saw or shaping with a router, you can add interest to plain surfaces. Layers of different woods can be laminated or joined in butcher block fashion, then cut and shaped for visual effect.

Inlay can be an art form in its own right. Delightful patterns of varying complexity and exactitude can be achieved with the proper tools and skill. At its simplest, shapes of different veneers are cut to

fit like a mosaic or puzzle and glued onto a base. The precision that machine-cut woods allow can be utilized in this and many other designs.

A few tips on safety. Operate all power tools with special care. Familiarize yourself with any appropriate safety techniques such as push sticks, jigs and feather sticks. Always wear eye protection and a dust mask when cutting or sanding. Ventilate your work space properly. Use common sense, and if you're unsure about something, don't try it. If you're tired, stop.

In the early twentieth century, some of the immigrants to America developed chip carving in the form of decorative boxes and furniture. Often called "tramp art," it was traded for essentials.

This frame is composed of many small wooden strips which have been notched with a whittling knife. The strips are then stacked in a pyramid fashion, nailed together with small brads, and fit at the corners. Each of the four sides is nailed to a slim wooden frame foundation which forms the rabbet.

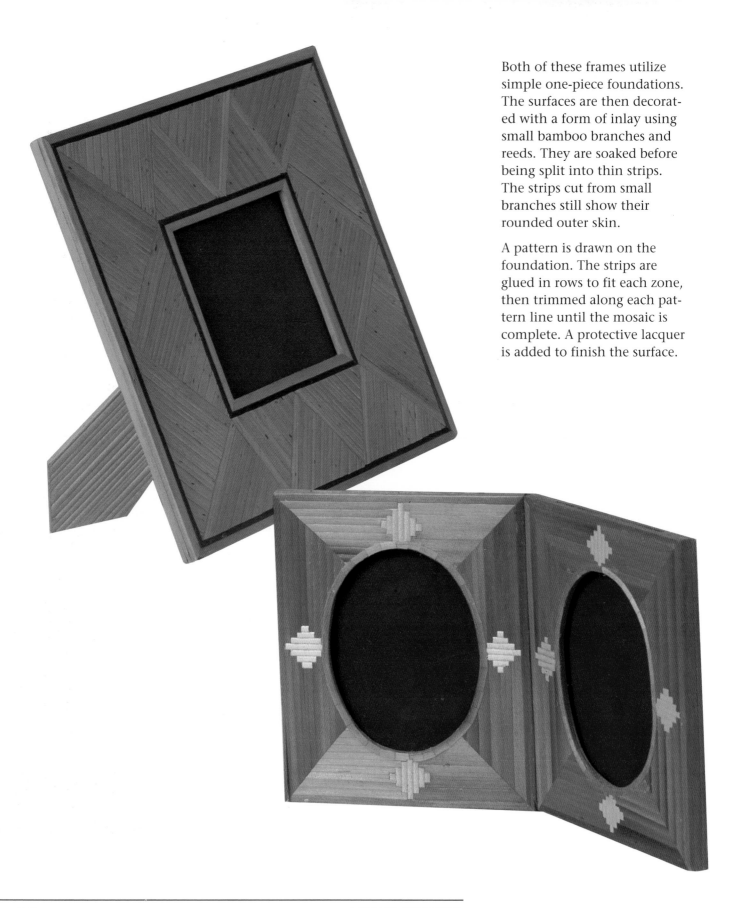

Both of these frames utilize simple one-piece foundations. The surfaces are then decorated with a form of inlay using small bamboo branches and reeds. They are soaked before being split into thin strips. The strips cut from small branches still show their rounded outer skin.

A pattern is drawn on the foundation. The strips are glued in rows to fit each zone, then trimmed along each pattern line until the mosaic is complete. A protective lacquer is added to finish the surface.

This is one of many possible variations on what has come to be known as a "Hicks frame." Edward Hicks was an American Quaker preacher and folk artist who popularized the raised square corner block. The block is usually of a contrasting wood or color from the frame, and can be flat, beveled, pyramided, routed with a reverse curve, painted, gilded, or whatever you like. The block can be simply glued on top of a frame, but is usually recessed like this one—sometimes with a lip that extends over the moulding.

The moulding can be joined with a conventional miter or a lap joint. The recessed area that accommodates the block can be cut out on a table saw and cleaned out with a chisel. Measure the size of the block from the outer tip of the moulding to determine the extent of the excavation. This frame features an outer rim which is not usually a part of Hicks frames.

The contemporary look of this walnut frame bespeaks elegant simplicity, but nonetheless requires some sophisticated technique. A table saw can cut the moulding and the triangular plates, but a versatile router is required to round off the corners. The last challenge is a considerable amount of hand sanding, though less if your wood is softer than walnut. The frame could be varnished, oiled or unfinished.

MILLED WOODS

Rip cut your moulding stock into the standard L-shaped cross-section to create a rabbet. Miter the corners as always. Measure and cut 45° sections from each end as shown here. Join the moulding.

Cut matching stock to conform to the triangular cutouts. Sand and fit, then glue and clamp them into place.

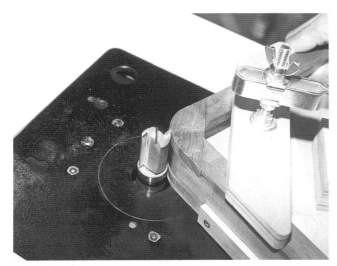

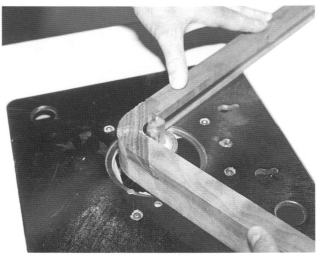

Using a router, round off the outside edges of each corner. Go slowly to achieve a smooth shape.

Carefully route out the inside edges of each corner. You may want to fit your blade with round jig to guide it.

Here's an ingenious freestanding frame that's easy to make. Cut the two triangular side panels out of solid stock. When stood upright, they should lean slightly back. Cut two same size panels of plexiglass that will sandwich your picture. Cut three equal lengths of medium size dowel and six short sections of small dowel for the lock pins.

Dado a groove, slightly wider than both plexiglass panels, parallel to the front edge of each wooden triangle. The groove should match the height of the plexiglass. Mark the three points for dowel holes: one just below the groove, one at the top and for-

Cherry and walnut strips were used to construct this distinctive frame. The ledge consists of two semi-circles of solid walnut. The joinery is straightforward and precise.

First make the inner frame by cutting a rabbet out of a walnut strip. Miter and join the corners. Measure the cherry strips to surround this inner frame. Mark all the regular intervals where the cherry will overlap. Dado out these zones to accommodate the width of strip halfway into each strip, then dado out the rabbets at the ends and corners. All the joints will lap equally, and can be glued and reinforced with nails from the back.

The edges of the ledge were routed. The shelf panel overlaps the wall mount panel, and is reinforced with dowel pegs from the top.

Any shapes can be used for a ledge, whether curved, rectangular or irregular. Many styles and decorative elements can be used. A groove can be cut to keep frames from sliding off.

NATURAL WOODS

True lovers of wood have a special appreciation for its raw form. Twigs, bark, split branches, weathered and worm-eaten grain evoke happy memories of woodland hikes and cozy cabins. Any picture displayed in such a frame is surrounded by a special warmth.

Consider barn siding or salvaged wood that has aged or weathered. It can also be adorned as a foundation with split twigs, strips of bark, vines and pine cones. Experiment with bamboo, driftwood, and oddly shaped branches. Collect natural materials that can be added as decoration, such as acorns, walnuts, gumballs, even mosses and fungi. A burly trunk can be cross-cut into a slab, and branches into small disks.

Take care when working with natural materials. Twisted grain can surprise a table saw and jump out of hand. Salvaged woods may have old nails or barbed wire that can ruin your blade. A dull whittling knife is a hazard. Allow green

wood to season after cutting to prevent warpage after assembly. Nail holes should be predrilled unless the wood is very soft. Inspect all materials for nesting insects that could damage the frame, the picture, or woodwork in your house.

Except for the hexagonal plywood foundation, this unique frame features all natural materials. First find the straight branch that will form the moulding. The thickness will determine how wide the plywood should be when you cut the center out of it. Paint the plywood. Rip cut about 1/3 the diameter of the branch away to create a flat bottom surface. Miter cut the six sections at 30° to whatever length you've chosen. Nail and glue these to the plywood.

Gather some vines, such as grapevine, and soak them overnight. Using small brads, tack them around the perimeter of the frame, twisting and braiding them as you go. Let dry. Hot glue an assortment of lichens and other woodsy materials all over the frame. This frame surrounds an arrangement of materials which is an extension of the frame itself, but you can frame anything you like.

You can find boards like these discarded at saw mills or sometimes lumber yards. The uneven edge could be outer bark or from a rotten center. If you have the tools, you can cut and plane sections of an old log. The trick to mitering the frame is to match the corners. A rabbet can be created either with a series of dado cuts or by adding strips at least 1/4" thick around the back.

Almost any scrap wood can be used for the moulding. This weathered barnwood has a rustic quality, but old clapboard, tongue-in-groove pine or even salvaged planks with peeling paint can be used effectively. Join the frame before drilling the holes through which the wire or twine will be laced. Different lacing patterns and ornamentation should also be considered.

Two rustic frames by Don Bundrick.

Cut the foundation shapes and their windows from solid 1" stock with a coping saw or jigsaw. Trace the mosaic pattern. Twigs will be cut to fit. The twigs used for these mosaics are cherry and mulberry. The large twigs are split in half, while the smaller ones are used whole. Boil twigs before bending them. Pre-drill the nail holes. Use brads that are slightly larger than the holes. Pictures can be mounted on thin plywood, then fastened behind the windows.

NATURAL WOODS

This design serves as an easel mount for a stock frame. The twigs you use must be straight. Attach rows of twigs one at a time by pre-drilling holes for long brads. Ends should be cut to shape after the rows are joined. When joining sections at perpendicular angles, pre-drill only partially, then drive several brads for a strong joint. Acorns and other ornaments can be attached with hot glue. The stock frame can be nailed to this easel assembly.

NATURAL WOODS

This grapevine treatment can be used to augment most any conventional frame. Begin by attaching four straight vine sections (see Fig. 1) to a frame with nails. These may be reinforced with glue. The corners should be lashed with tie wire, as will all the subsequent vine junctures.

Lash the four corner sections in place (Fig. 2), then add two or more long sections around the perimeter. A cross-brace should be attached at the mid-point of each side (Fig. 3). Wrap smaller vines around the outer members, then attach the curved pieces as shown in Fig. 4. You can soak or even boil vines to bend them more evenly.

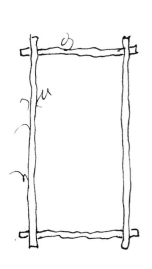

Figure 1

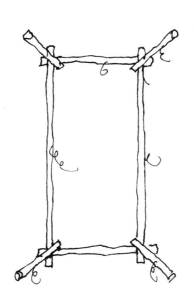

Figure 2

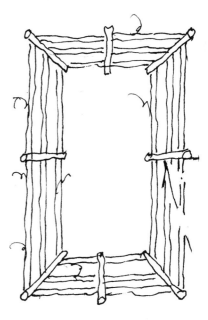

Figure 3

Figure 4

The ornate look of this easel is a natural result of the woodsy texture and delicate tendrils of the grapevine. First cut the three leg sections to an equal length. Drill a hole through the top of each and insert a bolt with a wing nut (see Fig. 1). Use tie wire to lash a horizontal piece across the front legs.

Add another piece or two with a bolt and nut to create a shelf (Fig. 2). Braid a small wreath-like ring with small vines, and a bow-like flourish with bent vines (Fig. 3). Vines can be soaked or boiled before bending and lashed with tie wire. Wire the ring and the flourish to the easel (Fig. 4), then wrap the lower front legs and shelf with small vines.

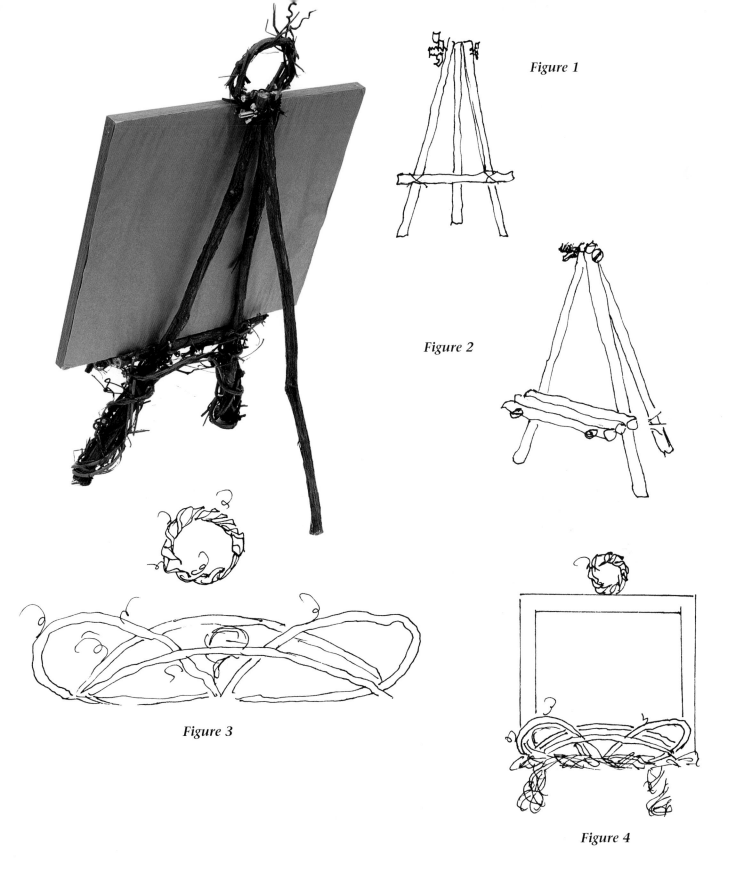

Figure 1

Figure 2

Figure 3

Figure 4

NATURAL WOODS

Here's a unique way to embellish a conventional frame. The sill incorporates a compartment at one corner that can serve as a planter for a live or dried arrangement. Other objects collected from nature can be used to decorate the sill.

Lash the first four sections of grapevine together with tie wire to fit the frame you wish to surround (see Fig. 1). Continue lashing parallel sections and cross-pieces to widen the framework (Fig. 2). Construct the sill the same width as the framework.

Lash the sill to the framework and add an angled brace at bottom right (Fig. 3). Construct and attach the basket-like compartment at bottom left. Weave small vines around the outer perimeter of the framework, the sill and compartment (Fig. 4). Weave medium size vines across the face of the framework and the edge of the sill.

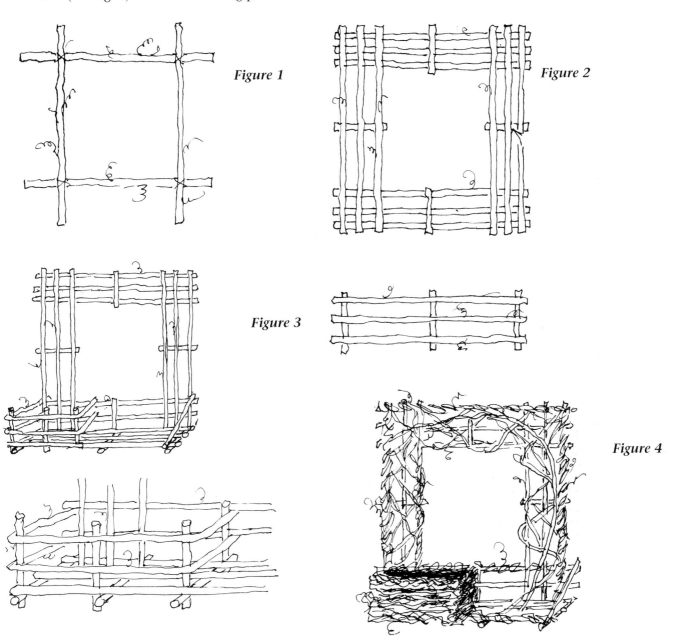

Figure 1

Figure 2

Figure 3

Figure 4

SHAPED & PAINTED WOODS

Wood is a wonderful material for making frames. It's available, affordable, and can be shaped in so many ways. Why be limited to the narrow range of traditional, commercial, assembly line mouldings? Wood can be sculpted.

Invest in some wide planks of solid pine or sheets of high grade plywood. Forget about linear moulding and think in two and three dimensions. Let the picture you wish to frame inspire the shape, texture and colors you choose. Sketch your ideas and be playful as you cut and arrange the components. One frame can lead to several variations.

Find a coping saw and a whittling knife. If you're motivated, get a jigsaw and carving tools to expand your capabilities. In addition to sculpting, you can also collect preshaped pieces like dowels, knobs, twigs, etc. The shapes you choose and make might be realistic or abstract, even mixed.

After shaping and sanding, prime and paint as you wish. Assembly can be done before or after painting, although unpainted wood will glue more securely. Larger components should be reinforced with nails or screws.

Whether you salvage the lathe-turned spires from an old piece of furniture or buy them new, the Gothic effect of this frame is surprisingly easy to achieve. The center panel can be cut from plywood. The base can be routed or layered. Large dowels form the sides, while standard moulding crowns the top. The piece is then painted gold and antiqued with speckles.

This hinged triptych is an old idea that still offers many possibilities. Imagine new shapes, styles, and subject matter. This design is freestanding, portable, and requires only plywood and hinges. A combination of decoupage and antiquing completes the effect.

51

The design possibilities of sculpting a free form frame out of plywood are limitless. Both the shape and the finish can be used to complement a subject however you wish.

Two-tone marbling accentuates this sculpted frame. The top layer adds dimension and interest as an inner border. The edges have been routed.

Here's a wonderful example of custom framing. The frame not only complements the subject in color, texture and motif, it becomes a literal extension of the subject. The frame, liner and grass panel were each cut from plywood sheets of varying thickness. Sponges were used for the multi-color finish.

SHAPED & PAINTED WOODS

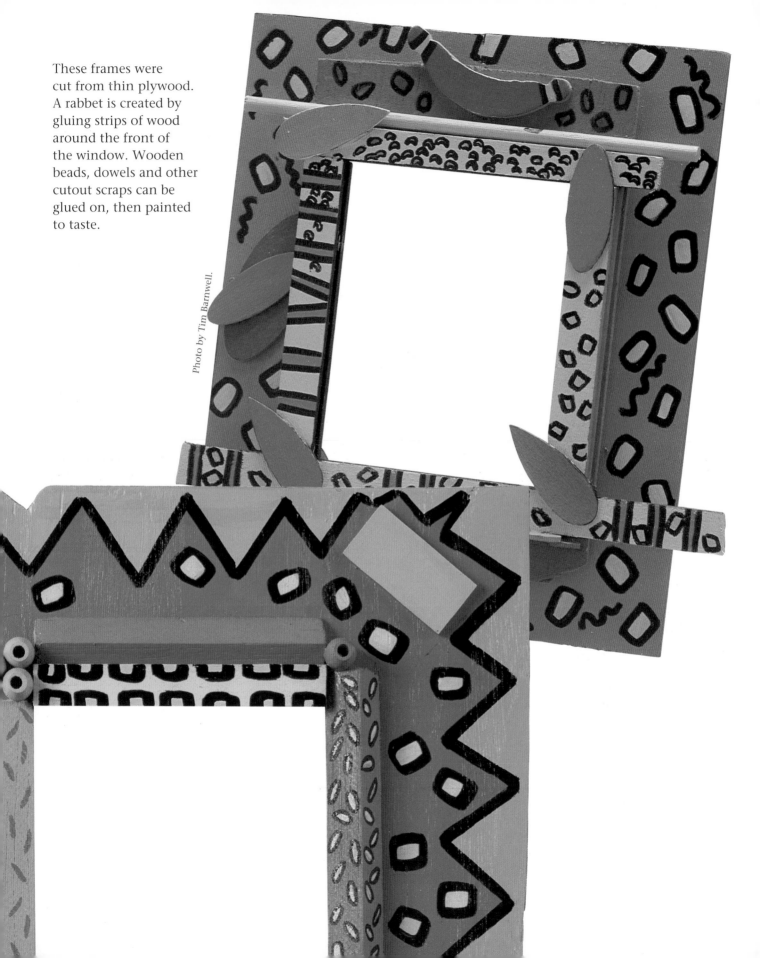

These frames were cut from thin plywood. A rabbet is created by gluing strips of wood around the front of the window. Wooden beads, dowels and other cutout scraps can be glued on, then painted to taste.

Photo by Tim Barnwell.

Standard square moulding is used for the frame foundation. Cabinet knobs are screwed in at the bottom corners. Plywood cutouts are glued and tacked at top and bottom, along with a curved twig. The surfaces are painted and decorated with glass beads, sequins or rhinestones, and scraps of fabric.

SHAPED & PAINTED WOODS

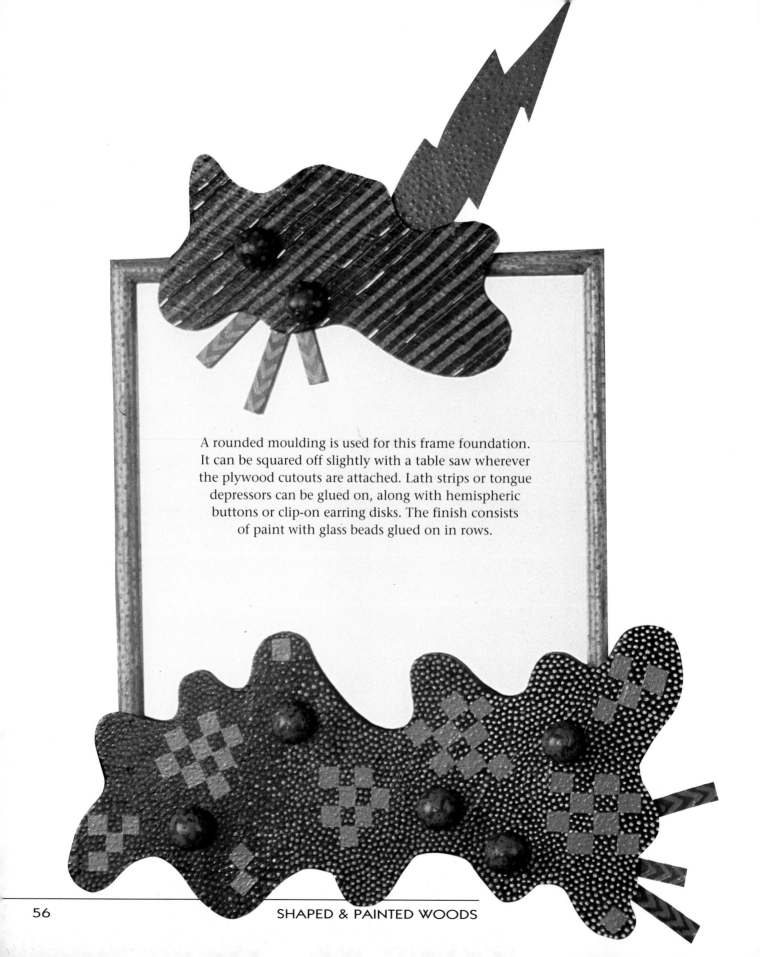

A rounded moulding is used for this frame foundation. It can be squared off slightly with a table saw wherever the plywood cutouts are attached. Lath strips or tongue depressors can be glued on, along with hemispheric buttons or clip-on earring disks. The finish consists of paint with glass beads glued on in rows.

SHAPED & PAINTED WOODS

Plywood cutouts are glued and tacked on to standard frames. Along with textured paint, glued on decorations include broken mirror shards, buttons, knobs, glass beads and fringe.

SPECIAL FINISHES

Any simple frame can be transformed into a spectacular work of art with just a little paint. From realistic images and stylized motifs to the rich palette of faux finishes, the real trick is to complement the picture being framed.

If the photo of your grandmother shows flowers in her hair, paint a few blossoms on your frame. For a landscape, paint leaves or ivy. Paint an architectural detail from the photo of an old house.

Be sensitive to the overall color scheme. With faux finishes, choose a texture that is complementary to the subject. Several specific techniques will be explained with the projects in this chapter.

Most of the finishes used in this chapter are created with various glazing techniques. Some are achieved by taping off areas and sponging or ragging the glaze. Others utilize more complicated manipulations of glazing through layering. Sometimes gilding precedes any glazing or detailing. A basic glaze can be made by mixing one part paint with equal parts of commercial glazing liquid and paint thinner.

SPECIAL FINISHES

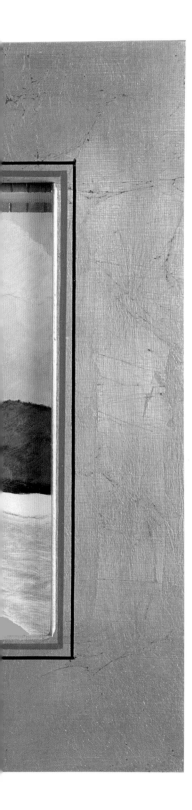

Due to the expense of real gold leaf, you may opt for faux gold, also known as composition gold or dutch metal, which is applied in much the same manner. To prepare a surface, apply 4-5 coats of oil base paint, then fine sand until very smooth. Red paint gives a warm glow to the gold and is also attractive as veins when gold is distressed. Next, apply a coat of gold size evenly wherever you plan to add gold. Allow the size to set about 18 hours before applying the gold.

You can remove each leaf of gold from its book using a gilder's tip, or with your fingers if you dust them liberally with talcum powder. Lay each leaf over the frame and press it gently on to the size with a soft sable brush or cosmetic brush until the entire area is covered. After the gold has set up for an hour or so, tap it down firmly with the brush, then force the excess gold off by pushing the brush at skewed angles. Finally, cotton wadding is dipped in hot water and rubbed all over the surface to remove any remaining flakes. Let it cure overnight. Protect faux gold with a clear coat of lacquer or varnish. Glazing or decorating can be added after this finish has dried.

If you want to distress the gold, hold off on the clear finish until you have done so. One method of distressing involves brushing on a glaze, allowing it to set up briefly, then rubbing it off so that some of the gold pulls away with it. Another way is to let thinner sit on the gold for a few seconds, then wipe it off with a rug. The thinner will open up any gaps or cracks in the gold, creating a linear pattern of veins.

This frame was first gilded, distressed and varnished. The area not to be glazed was then taped over. The pink glaze was brushed on, then a crumpled rag was pressed onto the glaze to create the pattern. The black pinstripes were added last.

This frame was created using the same process as the pink glazed frame. The only difference is that a sponge instead of a rag was used to create the pattern.

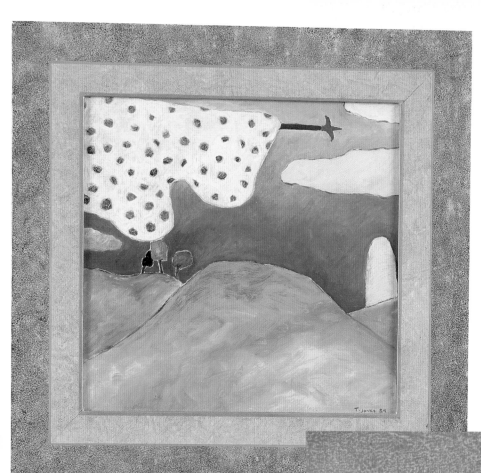

Both of these frames utilize sponging technique to texture the glazes. The light green band is the result of layering glazes. The gold bands are painted over top.

Here we start with two different base colors. The center band is taped off and painted dark green, then spattered with a slightly thinned oil paint consisting of black added to the dark green. The thinned paint is lightly loaded on to a stencil brush, then tapped against a stick on to the surface.

The surrounding bands are undercoated with red paint. Gold paint is then brushed on lightly, allowing some red to show through. After drying, it is lightly sanded to expose more red. Red paint is then mixed with some black and thinner to be spattered over the gold.

This faux maple is created in two steps. Over a medium yellow base, brush on a thin glaze of linseed oil, paint thinner and Japan dryers tinted with raw and burnt sienna artist oils. While still wet, impress it with a leather chamois that has been dampened and wrung out, then shifted over the glaze in an accordion fold. The glaze is then blended using a badger hair blender. As the glaze comes to tack, a dry brush is lightly loaded with a slightly darker glaze to add delicate grain lines.

After all this has dried, apply slightly darker glaze with the folded chamois. The outer edge is glazed darker and ragged. The inner band is faux gold leaf. The black rules are added with thinned paint on a lining brush against a straight edge.

Marbling begins with a base coat, in this case white. The center band is taped out, then a blue glaze is brushed on. The glaze is ragged, then veins are created by twisting a beveled rubber eraser across the surface. More veins are created by dipping a feather in thinner and jerking it across the glaze, then blotting lightly with a rag. After drying overnight, a second coat of glaze is brushed on to cut the contrast. The outer band is glazed during this second coat, and then it is ragged. The inner lip of gold is taped off, then rubbed on using a gold in wax compound.

Here we see two Hicks frames that have been marbled using different colors and degrees of patterning. There are many possible variations of marbling.

A tortoise shell effect can be created over a foundation of gold. Brush on a thinned oil stain of dark oak. Dab on varying shades of raw umber mixed with black. These are then blended outward using a badger hair blender.

SPECIAL FINISHES

These burl effects can be created with a linseed oil glaze similar to that described on page 65, although it is manipulated differently. Begin with a slightly more orange melon base color. Apply a glaze of sienna and ochre. A dry brush is used to add a darker version of this glaze for a wood grain effect, then blended with a badger hair blender. Study the grains of wood burl and play with this technique until you achieve the effect.

The ribbon banding on the outer edge is created by brushing on a medium brown glaze, adding darker shades at intervals, then blending outward with a dry brush. Remove most of the glaze before brushing to create the lighter areas.

FABRIC COVERINGS

Decorative fabric techniques are both diverse and very adaptable to framing. Almost any shaped frame foundation can be covered with a fabric treatment. In addition to cheap commercial frames, you should consider cutting out plywood or foam-core to your own unique specifications. These may be either covered directly or supplemented with foam rubber or other batting.

There are many fabrics to consider when wanting to create that special frame. Some are commercially available: textured, prints, brocades, satins, etc. Others may be procured from unique sources— even homespun, quilted, tie-dyed or batiked.

Embellishments can add a significant flair that completes your design. Consider color-coordinated braids, ruffles, ribbons and bows, woven tapes, lace and other artifacts. Fabrics can be stiffened with starches and lacquers. Imagine the possibilities.

72

Here's a straightforward approach to fabric covered frames. Strips of silk batik are spray mounted individually on to the moulding. Corners are trimmed and overlapped with a folded edge, then tacked at the back.

Spray paint a one-piece plywood frame cutout. This frame has a light spray of red over a white base coat. Cut out motifs from a printed fabric, or use iron-on patches, and affix to the frame. Embellish the images and surrounding space with textured paint.

FABRIC COVERINGS

This unique frame utilizes a plywood cutout foundation. The leaves and grapes have fiberfill batting sandwiches between double cutouts of green and purple. Stitch around the edges and then the veins. Wrap florist's wire with florist's tape for the stems. Insert one unwrapped end of the wire into each leaf and the grapes. The stems are attached to the plywood with duct tape or staples. Tendrils made of coiled florist's wire can be added the same way or inserted with the stems into the leaves. Strips of batting can be wound around the frame between the fastened leaves and grapes. Bias strips of brown fabric are wrapped around this and fastened at the back with staples.

Essentially, each of these three frames is upholstered. The foundation can be wide moulding, plywood, or even thick foam insulation board. Varying amounts of fiberfill batting are used for stuffing. Natural fiber fabrics, such as cotton, linen and wool, have enough elasticity that they can be shaped smoothly. Synthetics and blends tend to pucker when sewn, making them suitable for gathers and pleats. Be sure to cut fabrics on the bias to conform to the shape of the frame. These frames feature mitered corner seams and are custom fit much the way that upholstery is made to cover furniture. Fabric edges can be fastened to the back of the frame with staples and covered with heavy tape. Tack on wooden strips to create the rabbet.

This frame and liner are covered with lightweight China silk. Each has been hand-painted using silk paints with its own pattern. After covering both the frame and the liner, cut bias strips from the unpainted silk for piping. Sew enough strips end to end to cover a length of medium-thickness cording for the inner circumference of the frame. Fold over the cording and stitch close to the cord. Baste the piping to the frame, then insert the liner and tack it into place.

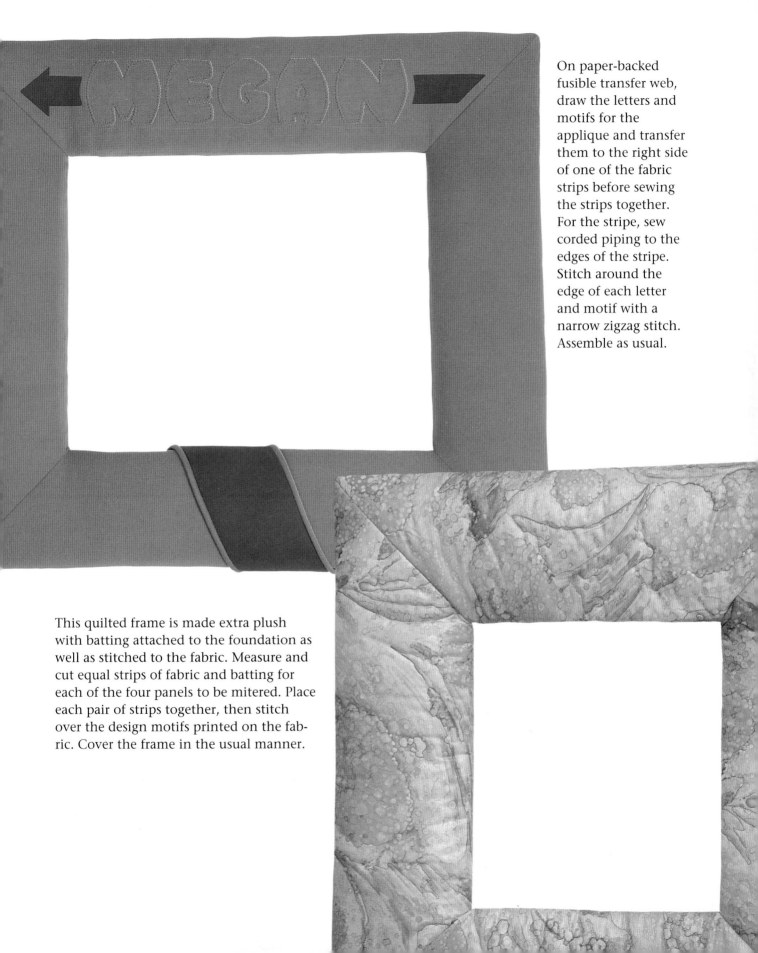

On paper-backed fusible transfer web, draw the letters and motifs for the applique and transfer them to the right side of one of the fabric strips before sewing the strips together. For the stripe, sew corded piping to the edges of the stripe. Stitch around the edge of each letter and motif with a narrow zigzag stitch. Assemble as usual.

This quilted frame is made extra plush with batting attached to the foundation as well as stitched to the fabric. Measure and cut equal strips of fabric and batting for each of the four panels to be mitered. Place each pair of strips together, then stitch over the design motifs printed on the fabric. Cover the frame in the usual manner.

For this distinctive frame use sisal rope, not nylon. The fibers will help hold the fabric strips in place. Cut long strips of cotton fabric about 2" wide on the cross grain for stretch-ability.

Tape the ends of the rope to prevent unraveling. Work on a flat surface, and use a pot or bowl to shape the first round of the coil. Begin and end the coil at the same point on the circle. Wrap the strips tightly around the rope. Tape the end of the strip firmly in place and cover the tape with the folded end of the new strip. At the beginning of the second round, then every 3" or 4", double the fabric strip and knot it around the previous row as shown in the drawing.

Make a bow and stitch it to the coil at the beginning/ending point. Glue the coils to a plywood foundation cut slightly smaller so as not to be visible from the edges.

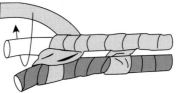

While this technique could be used with other fabrics and styles, we call this "the baroque bordello frame." Cut an oval of plywood. Use fabric that has some body, in this case tricot-backed metallic. Cut strips of fabric, on the cross grain, about twice the width of the frame. Strips should total in length about twice the frame's circumference. For the outer edge cut one strip, in width about four times the thickness of the frame, and in length the circumference of the frame plus 2".

Spread white glue over a portion of the frame at a time and let dry until tacky. Glue on one of the fabric strips, scrunching up the fabric as you go, leaving about 1/2" extending beyond the inner and outer edges of the plywood. Cover the end of each strip with the folded end of the next until the oval is complete. Glue the fabric edges down onto the inner and outer rims.

Fold and press one long edge of the narrow strip. Glue it around the outer rim, pinning if necessary. After it has dried, staple the raw edge to the back. Thick rayon cord is glued to the inner rim. Tack on a bow, and add faux gemstones with glue.

WOVEN MATERIALS

A variety of materials can be woven in different patterns to create appealing surfaces for frames. Some, like fabric strips, yarns or twines, will need to be wrapped over a foundation such as thin plywood or foam-core board. Others made of basketry materials will usually be stiff enough to hold their own shape.

Even though the woof and warp of most weaving implies a square or rectangle, you can explore other shapes for your frame. Whether curved or geometric, there really are no limits. A frame can celebrate all three dimensions.

Find colors and textures to weave that complement the subject you will frame. Ornamental objects can be woven into your design to further tie in with a motif, such as sea shells or jewelry.

Cigarette packs are folded and woven into this attractive double frame.

80

All sorts of reeds, vines or mixed strands can be used to braid this frame. The size, shape and embellishments can be varied as well. In this case, a #3 round reed was used.

Cut twelve equal lengths half again as great as your intended circumference. Soak them in warm water until they are flexible. Clamp them parallel to each other, then braid them in an arc in groups of four. The finished end is then inserted into the starting end, with each group of four meshing with its corresponding group. Clip off the ragged ends, clamp and let dry. Glue the splice and let dry before removing the clamp.

You could braid two equal ovals, sandwich clear acetate and tie them together, or glue one oval to a plywood cutout foundation. The top loop is made by inserting a length of soaked reed through the braid and winding it around itself into a tight circle, then back into the braid.

Borrowed from basketry, this basic design has lots of potential for variation. The frame shown here is woven using 3/8" flat reed.

For this 5" x 7" frame, cut 6 lengths at 21" and 6 at 31". Mark the centers of all of the pieces on the rough side of the reed with a pencil. Soak for a few minutes. Lay the 6 longer pieces vertically in front of you, three to your right and three to your left,

leaving a 4-3/4" space between them. The rough side of the reed should be facing you. Next you will be weaving the horizontal spokes, 3 spokes on the top and 3 spokes on the bottom of the vertical spokes. Leave a 6-3/4" space between the top and bottom spokes. Use the "over, under" method and alternate each row. The center marks will be in the center of the frame opening.

To weave the corners, mark the bottom of each set of three vertical spokes 1,3,5 and each set of the horizontal spokes 2,4,6. Repeat for the top corners. Place spoke 1 over all other spokes. Now take spoke 2 and lay it over spoke 1. Next take spoke 3 and lay it over spoke 3. Take spoke 4 and weave under spoke 1 and over spoke 3. Take spoke 5 and weave under spoke 2 and over spoke 4. Now take spoke 6 and weave over spoke 1 and under spoke 3 and over spoke 5. This completes one corner. Repeat for the rest of the corners. If your spokes are too long when you weave from corner to corner bury them behind a spoke, then hold them in place and cut to correct size.

To weave the sides, cut 44 spokes each 8" long. Weave each one separately with the smooth side (right side) facing you. Flip the frame over to bury each spoke end. This is considered one row. Work your way around the frame until you have completely filled the open space. Pack each row tightly against the previous one. There should be twelve rows on each long side and ten rows each on the top and bottom.

The frame can be stained once it has dried. It can be glued to a plywood foundation, or attached to a woven back with hook-and-loop tape (as shown here) with acetate sandwiched in between.

The basket frame can be decorated many ways, especially with natural materials like these dried flowers and Spanish moss.

WOVEN MATERIALS

Here's a technique that involves more winding than weaving. For a 5" x 6" oval frame you will need 3 ounces of longleaf pine needles, 20" of 16 gauge wire, 7 yards of 4-ply cotton thread and some beeswax. A No. 19 tapestry needle, a clothespin and a pair of scissors will also be used.

Trim pine needles just beyond the sheath (see Fig. 1). Pine needles may be used in their natural state or dyed with household fabric dye. Shape the wire into a 3-1/4" x 3-3/4" oval using the wire doubled.

Select a group of pine needles about 3/8" in diameter and lay them, blunt ends to the right, along one long side of the oval. Tie one end of a 36" length of thread to the wire and wrap the pine needles, right to left and over and under, keeping 1/4" between wraps. Add pine needles as necessary to maintain the 3/8" diameter coil by sliding them one by one into the coil (Fig. 2).

When one complete coil is achieved, clip the clothespin to the work. This will free your hands in order to thread the tapestry needle (Fig. 3). Working from back to front, stitch through the first wrapped

coil. This begins the stitching pattern. Every stitch hereafter will pass through the corresponding stitch in the previous coil (Fig. 4).

To give the frame depth, build the coils on top of, and slightly outside of, each other. Five complete coils should give the frame sufficient depth. Work outward for two more coils and then begin curving toward the back. Work two coils behind the level of the first coil (the one on the wire), and then work one coil inside the last coil. This final coil will hold the matboard backing in place (see Fig. 5).

Helpful hints: running each length of thread over beeswax will help ease it through the work without snarling. Colored thread can add even more interest to the finished frame.

Protect the frame with a light coat of hairspray for a matte finish. Trace around the frame on a piece of matboard, then cut it out for the backing. Cut a piece of acetate slightly larger than the window, insert your picture, then glue the backing to the frame.

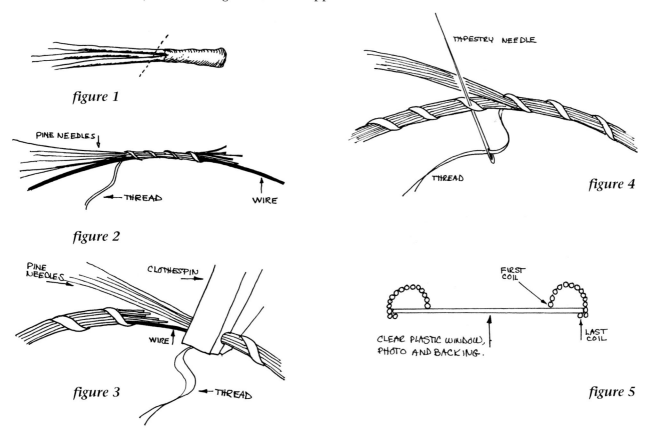

figure 1

PINE NEEDLES
THREAD
WIRE

figure 2

TAPESTRY NEEDLE
THREAD

figure 4

PINE NEEDLES
CLOTHESPIN
WIRE
THREAD

figure 3

FIRST COIL
CLEAR PLASTIC WINDOW, PHOTO AND BACKING.
LAST COIL

figure 5

PAPER TREATMENTS

Paper is an extremely versatile material with vast decorating potential. Papermaking is a fascinating craft in itself, and is accessible enough that you may want to fabricate your own materials from scratch. These can then be used to cover frames, liners and mats, or incorporated in other ways.

Papier-mâché expands the use of paper to sculpting in three dimensional form. You can mold your own design onto a simple foundation, or augment an old frame with some bas-relief.

Papers can be wrapped, wet or dry, around a frame and painted or lacquered. Papers can be crumpled to produce interesting textures such as faux leather when glued to the surface of a frame or liner.

Marbling is especially effective on paper. Whether you choose and coordinate the colors to marble yourself, or purchase paper already marbled, it can be utilized to enhance many styles of framing.

Decoupage is an easy technique that will enable you to dress up most any surface. Simply collect a range of paper materials (such as magazine clippings, wrapping paper, postage stamps, even leaves) and glue them to a foundation, then lacquer them.

Here's a great way to upgrade your refrigerator art. Cut any shapes you like out of matboard with a razor blade. The window is cut on three sides to leave a flap into which pictures are inserted. Use acrylic paints on all surfaces to seal and stiffen the matboard. A strip of magnetic tape is glued to the top of the back.

This lightweight accordion frame is easy to make and can be varied in shape and color. Find a stiff decorative paper (e.g. marbled, wallpaper, etc.) for the folds. The paper used to cover a foam-core foundation can either match or complement. Glue it on, cut an X in the window and wrap all edges. Strips of folded paper should exceed the circumference by 4-6 times. Corner strips should be cut as half doughnut shapes. Run glue down the bottom edge of each fold to attach each section.

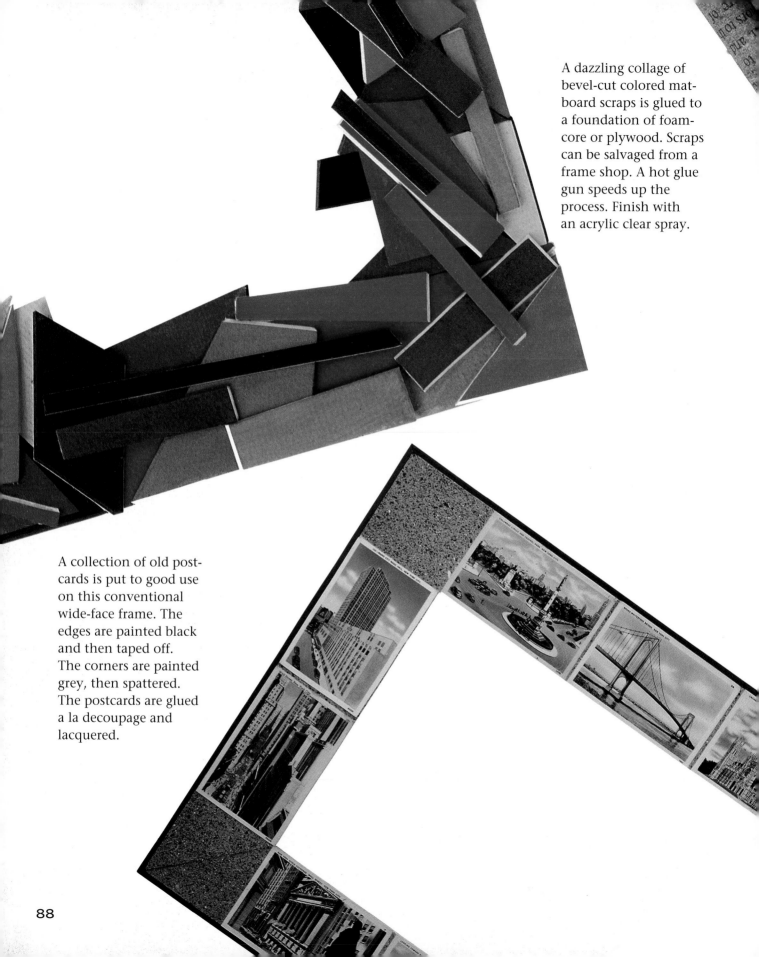

A dazzling collage of bevel-cut colored mat-board scraps is glued to a foundation of foam-core or plywood. Scraps can be salvaged from a frame shop. A hot glue gun speeds up the process. Finish with an acrylic clear spray.

A collection of old post-cards is put to good use on this conventional wide-face frame. The edges are painted black and then taped off. The corners are painted grey, then spattered. The postcards are glued a la decoupage and lacquered.

These tube mosaics are created simply by rolling newspaper around a pencil, chopstick or dowel, and gluing them to a foamcore or plywood foundation. Fasten the outer edge of the paper with white glue after rolling. Cut the ends as necessary to fit whatever pattern you have chosen. Tightly rolled paper can be patterned in intricate designs akin to inlay. Zones of color can also be varied.

This series of frames utilizes papermaking techniques. They are rather fragile and need to be glued to a foundation of plywood or thick foam-core that has a rabbet. In addition to pre-sized and beaten cotton pulp, you will need a piece of fiberglass screening, cardboard, pellon, a bucket and a sponge.

First decide the shape and size of your frame, then sketch it onto a piece of cardboard. Cut this out to use as a template. Cut a piece of pellon several times larger than your template. Lay the template down in the middle and trace the outline with a permanent marker onto the pellon. Lay the pellon on a waterproof work surface. Place the wet pulp within the outline on the pellon with your hands. Once you have filled the outline to a thickness of about 1/2", it's time to start pressing to remove the excess water.

Place a sheet of fiberglass screening over the pulp, and start applying gentle pressure with a sponge. Squeeze the excess water into a bucket. Apply more pressure as you proceed. If you want to imprint the pulp, position whatever objects you have chosen on the pulp before covering it with the fiberglass. If you want to texture the entire surface with something like a bamboo mat, put it beneath the pulp instead of the pellon. After pressing, the edges will be a little uneven. You can use a straight edge to gently shape the edge if you like. The objects used for imprinting can be left in place until the frame has finished drying, then removed.

The dried surface can be finished with a mixture of watered down white glue. You can add luster pigments to this mixture to add a little sparkle. These contain mica and can be obtained from most paper supply companies. Other paints can be brushed on or stamped on. You can carve your own stamps from a potato or gum eraser and stamp on ordinary poster paints. Children's blocks and other found objects can also be used for stamping.

For further embellishment, glue on objects such as buttons, beads, seeds, dried flowers, trinkets…whatever suits your motif. You can also mold small objects out of pulp using cookie cutters, candy molds or other concave shapes. Use the same pressing technique and let the castings dry in or out of their molds. Paint them and glue them on.

A few of the many objects you can use to mold and imprint wet paper pulp.

PAPER TREATMENTS

EARTHEN CASTINGS

Even if you've never thrown a pot in your life, you can have fun making a frame in this medium. For starters, there's plaster casting. Molds can be purchased or improvised. Keep these frames fairly small, and glue them to a foundation for strength. Finish them with paint and lacquer.

Salt dough is another option. With a simple recipe you can mold, sculpt and imprint your designs. Finish them as you would the plaster. The same applies to modeling clay.

Ceramics require more tools and expertise, but offer great design potential and extra durability. Other sorts of mixtures can be shaped into frames. Consider concrete, or sandpainting...

Mosaics lend themselves beautifully to the surface design of frames. In addition to titles, you can incorporate other ceramic fragments, broken china, pieces of mirror and glass, stones, bones, beads, coins, etc. Or roll clay into round strips, then piece different lengths and colors into a mosaic pattern.

All sorts of objects can be used for imprinting: woven textures, leaves, buttons, jewelry, machine parts, cut glass...virtually anything.

These small free form frames are easy to make.
Use a ceramic-like sculpting compound. Roll it
out to a thickness of about 1/4" with a rolling
pin. Cut to shape with a kitchen knife. Imprint
with objects, then bake in your oven (not
microwave) at 275°-290° F for 15-20 minutes on
a non-metallic plate. Cool 10 minutes, then
paint with tempera or acrylics. Magnetic tape
can be glued on the back for refrigerator art.

You can use self-hardening or oven bake clay for
these circles. Roll out to a thickness of 1/2" thick,
then cut to shape. They can be molded inside a
curved saucer and turned by hand. Paint and glaze
as you wish.

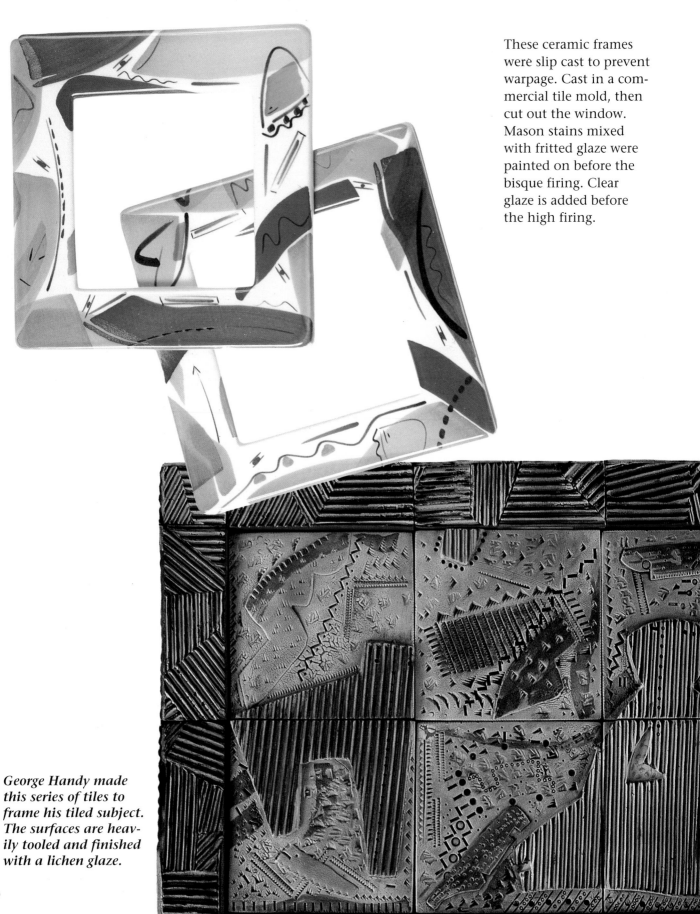

These ceramic frames were slip cast to prevent warpage. Cast in a commercial tile mold, then cut out the window. Mason stains mixed with fritted glaze were painted on before the bisque firing. Clear glaze is added before the high firing.

George Handy made this series of tiles to frame his tiled subject. The surfaces are heavily tooled and finished with a lichen glaze.

Mosaic technique offers a wide range of design potential. Start with a one-piece plywood foundation. Glue and nail on a lip of 1/4" wooden strips around the inside and outside edges. Paint.

Pour a plaster mix grout, which you can color to taste, into this recess. Press fragments of shattered earthenware, china, porcelain, glass or what have you into the grout. Smooth out the seams and let dry. Sturdy hangers will be needed to support the weight.

This reproduction of an antique frame looks like it's been carved in stone. The first step in this process is to find a frame to serve as your model. Build a box around it, then pour a two-part polyurethane mixture over the model. It will set up like rubber to serve as your mold.

There is an assortment of non-firing casting mixtures from which to choose. Many are plaster mixes intended for molding. One of these (hydrostone) was used to make this frame. There are also various sorts of polyesters and acrylic resins. If your piece is thick enough (3" or more), you can even use concrete. Some pieces may need wire or fiberglass reinforcing inside.

Colors can be added to the casting mix in the form of paints, powders, colored sand, etc. Metal filings can be added, then oxidized with acids for effect. Sandblasting is a good way to texture the surface. The piece can be dipped in clear casting resin or it can be painted on.

These wonderful ceramic frames by Kathy Triplett were inspired by the juxtaposition of organic insect and sea creature forms with the angularity of futuristic machine-like pieces.

STAINED GLASS

Because of the translucence of these frames, you'll want to display them in a window or on an easel near a lamp. While the subjects in the frames shown here are permanently sealed, heavy wire could be crimped in the back to hold a removable plate. You might also want to execute a design that is more three dimensional, or incorporate stained glass panels into a wooden or metal frame.

Stained glass joinery takes a little practice, but here are some basics to get you started. Draw your pattern to scale. Cut each piece in place over the pattern, leaving a 1/16" gap between all edges. Clean the glass before wrapping the edges with copper foil tape. Paint "paste flux" over all foil. Place the tip of the soldering iron to the foil, then the tip of some 50-50 solid core wire solder next to it until it flows. Run solder around all the foiled edges. Place pieces together, touch both adjacent edges with the iron tip and run solder into all the seams. To touch up rough spots,

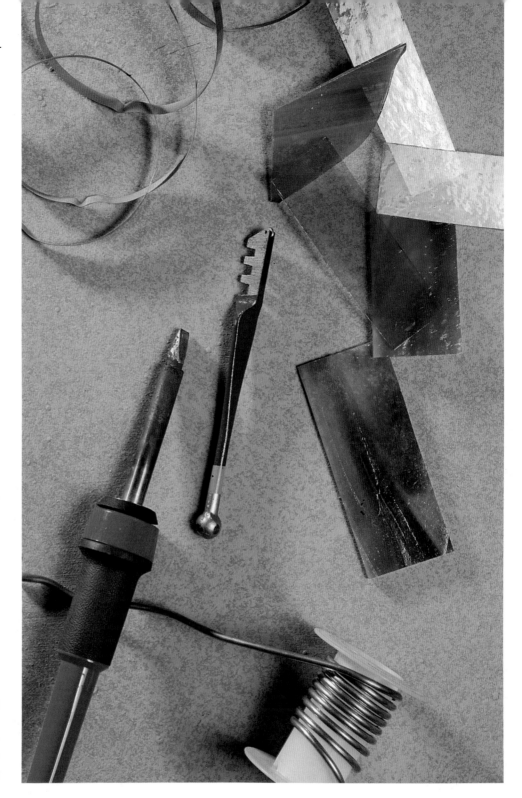

paint on flux, then run the iron and solder down the seam as necessary to form a smooth rounded bead. Keep the iron moving to prevent the solder from dripping through the other side. Clean all seams with dishwashing liquid and water. Short lengths of heavy wire can be soldered as loops in the back or top edge for hanging.

Family photos, wedding and birth announcements can be enhanced with flowers or other moments in these permanently sealed frames.

Mr. and Mrs. James A. Leonard
and
Mr. and Mrs. Gary I. Heidlebaugh
invite you to share in the joy
of the marriage uniting their children
Jennifer Lee
and
Brant William
The two shall become one
Saturday, the twenty-seventh of June
nineteen hundred and ninety-two
at eleven-thirty in the morning
Laguna Vista Estates
Heron Lake, New Mexico

STAINED GLASS

Each of these three frames can be made using only straight cuts. The diamond is a pre-cut beveled pane. The black chevrons around the lavender frame are soldered on to the thick lead came as a top layer, while the rest of the piece is foiled.

All of these frames require curved cuts. They also utilize a technique where excessive solder is applied to form decorative beads. Semi-precious stones and a flamingo brooch are incorporated into the designs.

MOTIFS IN METAL

Metals are diverse in appearance and malleability. Depending on the material, joining techniques can involve crimping, screwing, bolting, gluing, soldering or welding. Metals can create spectacular visual effects and should not be overlooked just because the techniques may seem formidable.

Metal foils can be glued over simple foundations or old frames. Crumpling beforehand produces an attractive veined texture. Metal hardware, trinkets or other objects can be glued, tacked or screwed on as further decoration.

Tin or other soft metal sheeting can be shaped into frames or over a foundation. Surfaces can be punched or raised into patterns. Edges can be cut and bent to create dramatic borders.

Copper tubing, plumbing fittings, metal fixtures, hardware, coins and other objects can be fastened together without welding. Of course, if you want to weld and work with heavier metals, your design options will increase all the more.

*Tinted copper tubing is beautifully wrought for
the bamboo effect of this frame by Andy Brinkley.*

Here's a metal project geared for the novice. Hammer a copper pipe on a hard, even surface until it is flattened. Draw a line down the center with a felt tip marker. Cut with a hack saw two lengths at 6" and two at 6-1/2" (or as you prefer). Center punch and drill a 3/16" hole 1/2" from each end of all four pieces. Hammer marks with a nail punch and a screw driver tip down the center lines to make a design.

Cut a 5-3/8" x 5-7/8" rectangle of thin plywood or masonite for the backing. Line up the holes in the copper over the backing and drill through. Cut a rectangle of plexiglass to fit inside these four points. If using glass, add rubber washers between the copper and glass to prevent cracking.

Polish the copper with steel wool and paste wax, or finish with a clear polyurethane spray to prevent tarnishing. Line up the backing, picture, glass and copper, then join with brass nuts and bolts.

MOTIFS IN METAL

This recycled tin has been cut, folded and punched into a box-like frame. Borrowing from stained glass joinery, the edges of the glass panels are covered with crimped strips of tin and soldered to the metal framework. Edges of the tin are crimped and soldered to adjacent panels. The shadow box and hinged door are rather elaborate, but you might opt for a more two-dimensional design. Slits and patterns can be cut or torched. Strips can be cut and twisted. Tin is very malleable.

These elegant metal frames are wrought using salvaged steel from a junkyard, and require some experience with welding. Metal sheers and a band saw will prove useful in cutting out many of the shapes. A small welding tip, such as a jeweler's tip, is also recommended for some of the detailing.

The frame is made of L-shaped strips for a ready-made rabbet. Four sections of 1/8" round stock (wire) is braided for one of the frames. The coloration occurs naturally due to different metals and thicknesses interacting under fire. Finish with a clear spray lacquer to prevent further oxidation. The strength of these frames makes them ideal for supporting heavy artwork.

One-of-a-kind frames of hand embossed pewter,
ornamented with stones, by Jenny Jotic.

MOTIFS IN METAL

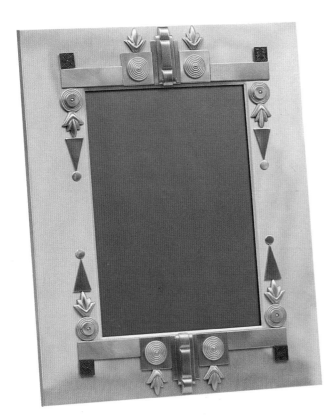

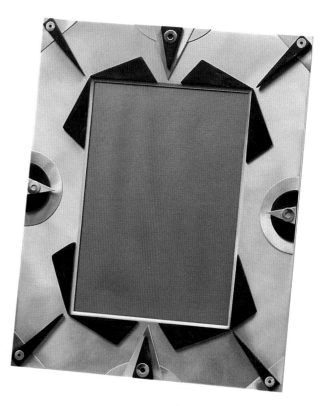

Distinctive handmade designs by Allison Stern incorporating metals, plastics, fiberglass, and recycled technological components.

MOTIFS IN METAL

FOUND OBJECTS

The only limit here is your imagination. Although you may want to create a frame using one object exclusively (buttons, shells, feathers, etc.), it's difficult to resist the mixed media approach. When you think of all the tantalizing possibilities…

Unless you're framing a mirror, you'll probably want to assemble a range of objects that are related to your framed subject. The relationship could be one of color, texture, shape, or thematic association. You could add a concise arrangement at one corner of a simple frame, or cover every square inch with festoonery.

Chances are you'll begin with a functional frame as a foundation. This is a great way to utilize an otherwise unattractive frame. If you prefer to increase your design options, it's easy to cut a simple one-piece foundation any shape you like out of plywood. You can paint the foundation before or after attaching other materials, depending on your design. Objects can be fastened with glue, nails, screws or tied on.

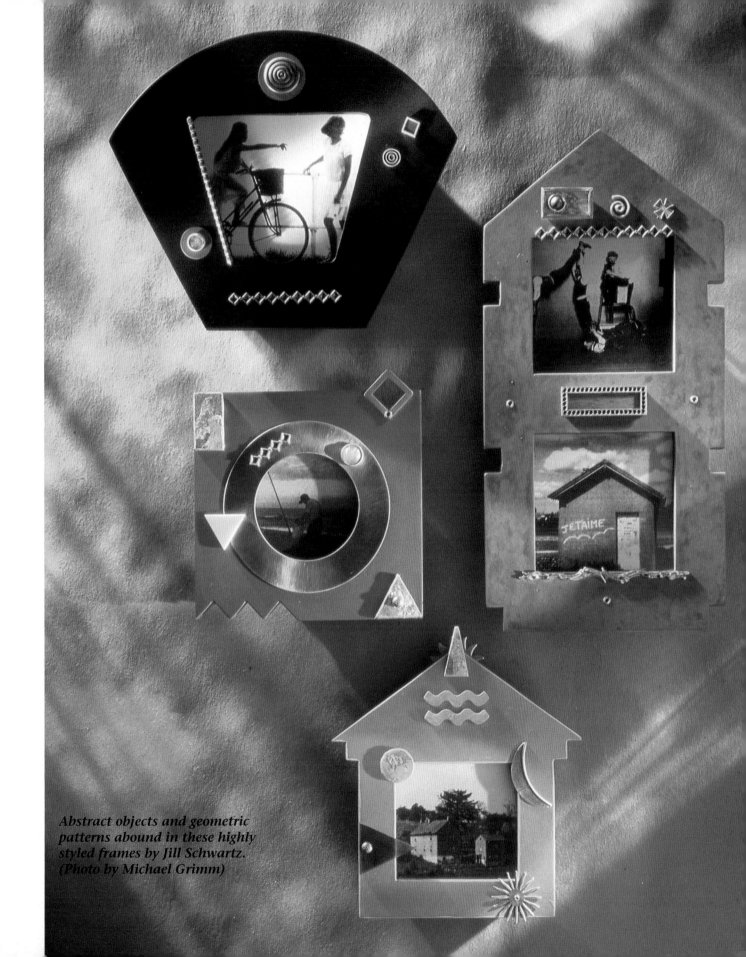

Abstract objects and geometric patterns abound in these highly styled frames by Jill Schwartz. (Photo by Michael Grimm)

Buttons and lace transform these ordinary frames into keepsakes worthy of your grandmother's dressing table. You may want to cover the frames in velvet before gluing on the ornaments.

One of these frames is covered with suede, the other with soft leather. Spray adhesive is used for even hold, then a latex cement secures the edges to the back with a few staples for reinforcement. Feathers are then glued on in dazzling clusters using white glue.

This spectacular frame resonates with the design elements of its subject. The glitter paper has a peel-off adhesive backing. Strips and shapes are cut out with pinking shears, then simply stuck on the foam-core foundation.

Old 35mm slides are recycled into this striking mosaic. They are sprayed with enamel paints, glued to a foam-core foundation, then decorated with enamel paint markers.

This dramatic effect is created with inexpensive fans and spray paints. Lay fans, slightly open, on a matboard. Spray paint them lightly. Move them around and spray with different colors, creating patterns on the matboard. Cut the matboard into a frame shape, glue it to a matching piece of foam-core, the glue the fans on. Decorate further with metallic markers.

Start with a traditional concave mitered frame. Colored pearls are glued on randomly. Glass bugle beads are glued on in rows to fill in. You may want to thread them over thin wire to speed up the process. The outside edge is a row of globular metallic beads. The outermost fringe is optional.

Photos by David Luttrell.

FOUND OBJECTS

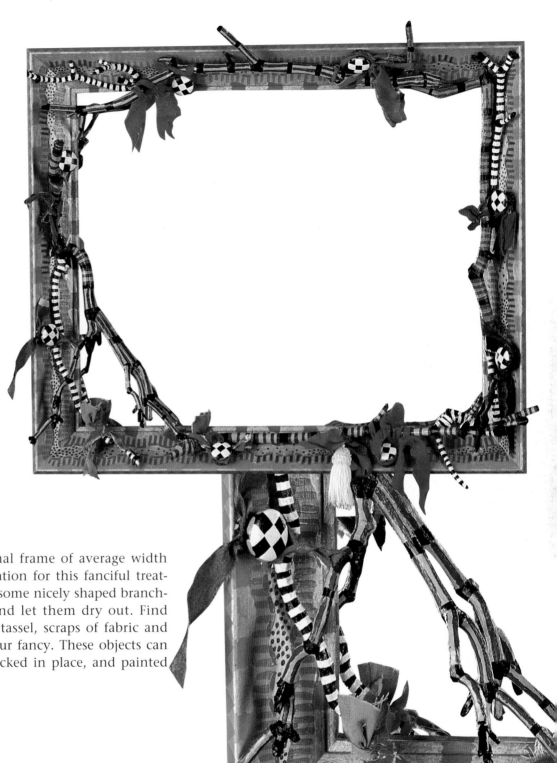

Almost any conventional frame of average width can serve as the foundation for this fanciful treatment. Collect and trim some nicely shaped branches. Remove the bark and let them dry out. Find some cabinet knobs, a tassel, scraps of fabric and whatever else strikes your fancy. These objects can be glued, screwed or tacked in place, and painted before or after assembly.

FOUND OBJECTS

SHADOW BOXES

The function of these frames is to be deep enough to contain a three-dimensional subject. They can be open, sealed, or have a hinged panel so that subjects can be changed.

This is an excellent way to display memorabilia or collectibles. If you intend to change the subjects periodically, you may choose a style of frame that is integrated with your interior decor. Shadow boxes sometimes function essentially as display cabinets or knick-knack shelves. They are nonetheless a framing variation that afford a unique opportunity for creativity.

With a deep enough frame you can create space for a three-dimensional display. This frame was painted with enamel markers in a sawtooth quilt design to complement the subject.

From 1/2" ply or solid stock, cut 8 equal panels for this open frame. Slots are cut halfway through each panel where they intersect. Join with glue and nails. Plywood cutouts for the fish, eye, palm tree and stars are glued and nailed on. Glue on jewels and tail fringe, then paint.

Start with mitered panels for a deep frame. Mount artwork on a back panel and attach with glue and nails. Cut an equal front panel with an oval window. Cut out a same size piece of fiberfill batting and spray mount it to the front panel. Cover with fabric, fastening with staples on the back. Glue this to the frame, with a few tiny brads for reinforcement. A dried floral arrangement anchored in a styrofoam block is inserted.

SHADOW BOXES

This classic hinged shadow box is constructed primarily with solid 1" x 4" stock. Miter the corners to size, then rip cut 1" away for the glass door section. Join both frame sections, then glue and nail on a back panel. Miter and join a conventional mould-ing of equal size. Cut glass to fit. Glue and nail these to the door frame. Finish with stain or paint as you wish. Attach the door with two butterfly hinges. The inside can include shelves if you like, so you may display whatever you want.

SHADOW BOXES

These shadow boxes illustrate just how effective a three-dimensional display can be. There's an abstract dollhouse miniaturization at work here that would not exist without the dynamics of deep framing. Notice how the subjects are contained and enhanced by the fully dimensioned use of matboard inside the frame. Think of all the subjects you might want to display in this sort of full proscenium stage.

R.Vincent Smith

SHADOW BOXES

MATS & LINERS

Matting provides an effective way of extending and enhancing the border of a frame. Liners are literally an extension of the frame, and particularly adapted for framing oil paintings. Mats are generally enclosed under glass.

Mats can be cut with any shape of window that complements the subject. A pattern of multiple windows is also effective. Patterns can be cut in the top mat to reveal a different colored mat below. Mats can be scored with V-cut patterns, or even inlayed. Decorative borders can be added with ink, paint or tape. A beveled window can be cut out of extra thick foam-core, then covered with thin paper for a sumptuous effect.

Mats can be painted with patterns and motifs, or decorated with ribbons or other flat objects. Decorative papers, such as color samples, wrapping papers or marbled papers, can be cut into patterns and glued on top of a mat. Fabrics and other materials can also be used to cover a mat.

While painting a mat, why not do the frame to match? These were decorated with spray paints applied in many layers over stenciling objects.

Wrap the frame with ribbon and any type of netting. Spray two or more colors from different angles. Shift the stencils if you wish. For the mat, stencil with paper cutouts, doilies, fancy ribbon, netting…whatever you like. Keep adding colors and layers for the effect you want. Cut the window bevel clean for a finished look.

Here's a fine example of matting technique. Color coordinated wrapping paper is mounted on the back board, with the record attached over top. Four successive mats with variable margins are laid over this. The top mat is scored with a V-cut pattern that adds interest and style.

MATS & LINERS

This commercially available matboard has a textured fabric bonded to it. You might choose to
mount your own fabric on a matboard. The twelve-
sided window creates a nice border tension while
complementing the shape of the batik.

This technique adds texture and pattern with a range of color. Brush a thick coat of iridescent paint on a black matboard. Cut a wide-tooth comb out of a matboard scrap. Drag the comb through the wet paint in wavy lines or other patterns. Let dry, then add accent lines with enamel markers.

132

Start with a black or navy blue mat. Using light blue enamel spray paint, lightly mist part of the mat. Mist a little more of the mat with white spray paint, then depress the nozzle very lightly to drip larger dots of white. Cut the window. Affix glow-in-the-dark stickers and outline them with glow dimensional paint.

A thick coat of faux granite paint is sprayed on this black mat. A blunt object, such as a screwdriver, spatula or butter knife, is used to scratch patterns through to the black. Let dry, then accent with colored inks or paint markers.

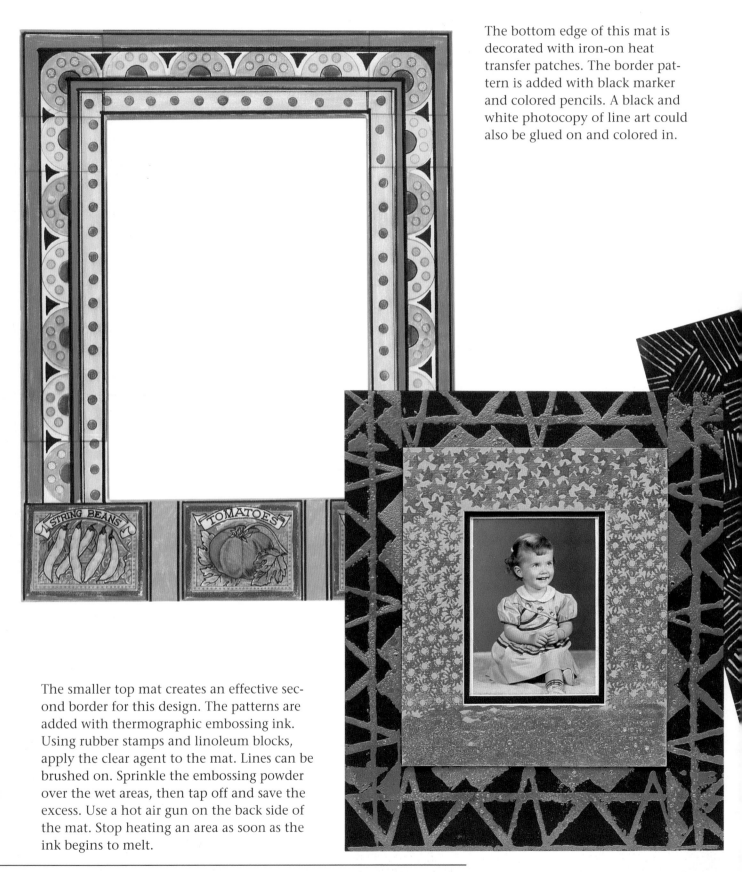

The bottom edge of this mat is decorated with iron-on heat transfer patches. The border pattern is added with black marker and colored pencils. A black and white photocopy of line art could also be glued on and colored in.

The smaller top mat creates an effective second border for this design. The patterns are added with thermographic embossing ink. Using rubber stamps and linoleum blocks, apply the clear agent to the mat. Lines can be brushed on. Sprinkle the embossing powder over the wet areas, then tap off and save the excess. Use a hot air gun on the back side of the mat. Stop heating an area as soon as the ink begins to melt.

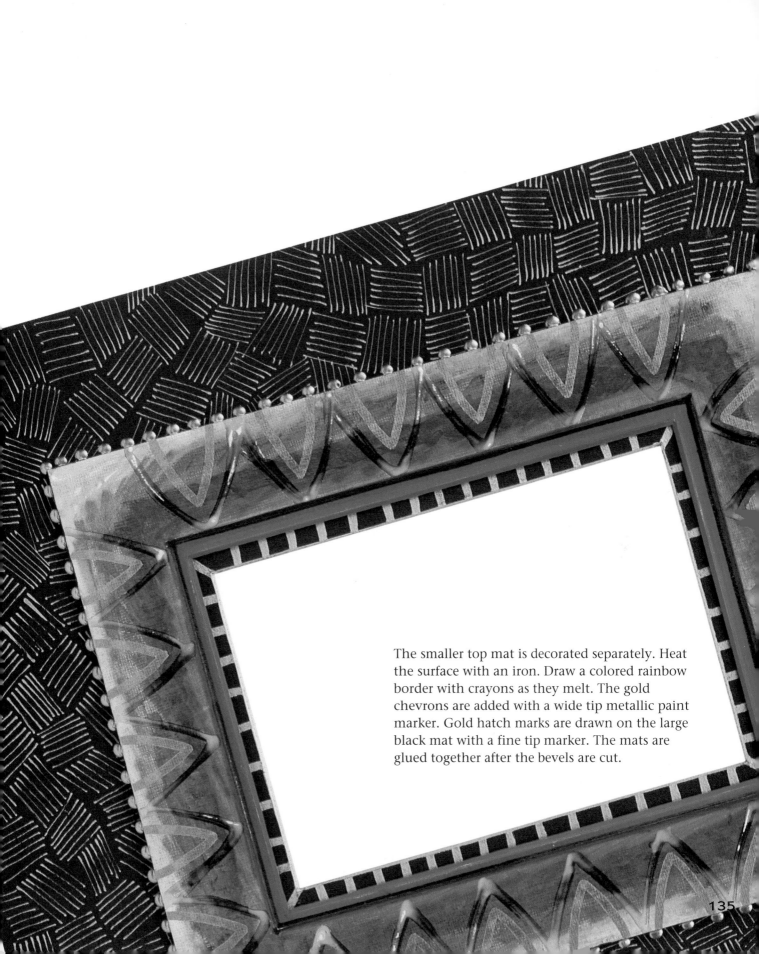

The smaller top mat is decorated separately. Heat the surface with an iron. Draw a colored rainbow border with crayons as they melt. The gold chevrons are added with a wide tip metallic paint marker. Gold hatch marks are drawn on the large black mat with a fine tip marker. The mats are glued together after the bevels are cut.

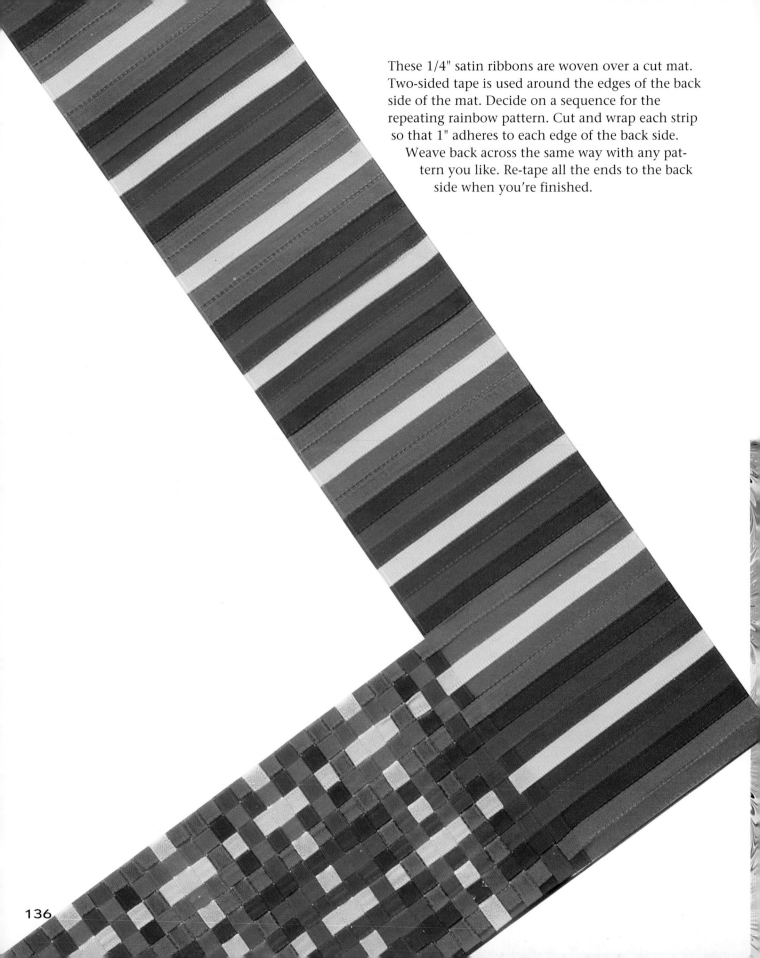

These 1/4" satin ribbons are woven over a cut mat. Two-sided tape is used around the edges of the back side of the mat. Decide on a sequence for the repeating rainbow pattern. Cut and wrap each strip so that 1" adheres to each edge of the back side. Weave back across the same way with any pattern you like. Re-tape all the ends to the back side when you're finished.

Marbled paper adds richness and flair to most any mat treatment. It can be simply spray mounted on to a matboard, then bevel cut as usual. Or it can be wrapped around a pre-cut mat and fastened to the back just the way fabric is done.

The accordion fold follows the same basic procedures explained on page 87. Fold and glue the corners first, then fill in with the wedge-shaped sides. This mat will need spacers to raise the glass.

Here's a unique way to add color and texture to a mat. Different materials are sprinkled on to a surface that has been painted with glue. The smallest mat uses crayon shavings, perfect for a child's drawing. The largest features lavender with miniature rosebuds, while the other boasts a potpourri of saffron, parsley, coriander and mustard seeds, bay leaves and allspice berries. These could frame a favorite recipe in your kitchen. Use spacers to raise the glass above these mats.

MATS & LINERS

A continuous sheet of tree bark is removed from a fallen tree (don't strip a live one!), then soaked and pressed until flat. It is glued to a thin foam-core sheet. Windows can be cut out with a fine-tooth coping saw. If the bark is flaky, seal it with a clear polyurethane spray.

The wide liner panels shown here have been covered with a variety of materials to complement their subjects: printed fabric, wallpaper, wrapping paper and vinyl leatherette.

MATS & LINERS

These liners feature
faux marbling and a
sponged antique gold
(see chapter on Special
Finishes).

MATS & LINERS

ARTIST'S DIRECTORY

Thomas Beaman
(page 108)
171 Bull Creek Rd.
Asheville, NC 28805

Andy Brinkley
(page 107)
Rt. 8, Box 1482
Hickory, NC 28602

Don Bundrick
(page 41)
P.O. Box 84
Tallulah Falls, GA 30573

Dawn Cusick
(page 138)
P.O. Box 984
Clyde, NC 28721

Don Daniels
(pages 44-49)
Rt. 2, Box 889
Locust Grove, OK 74352

Fred Gaylor
(pages 21, 39, 51, 88, 97,
   122, 124, 125, 130, 131,
   140-142)
P.O. Box 254
Burgaw, NC 28425

George Handy
(page 96)
2 Webb Cove Rd.
Asheville, NC 28804

Bobby Hansson
(page 42)
P.O. Box 1100
Rising Sun, MD 21911

Beverly Harang
(pages 81-83)
370 Sondley Dr. East
Asheville, NC 28805

Michael Hester
(pages 37, 40)
244B Swannanoa River Rd.
Asheville, NC 28805

Jenny Jotic
(page 112)
859 East Jeffrey St.
Apt. 502
Boca Raton, FL 33482

Heidi Kimsey
(page 116)
208 Pearson Dr.
Asheville, NC 28801

Claudia Lee
(pages 90-93)
317 Cumberland St.
Kingsport, TN 37660

Mary Jane Miller
(pages 40, 87, 89, 137)
Rt. 3, Box 900
Abingdon, VA 24210

Marty Mitchell
(pages 101-105)
c/o T.O.G.
421 Haywood Rd.
Asheville, NC 28806

Baker Moorefield
(pages 6, 55-57, 120,
   121, 123)
505 Forest Hills Blvd.
Knoxville, TN 37919

Barry Olen & Jenifer
Patterson
(page 117)
c/o Wings
19 Wall St.
Asheville, NC 28801

Beth Palmer
(pages 54, 87, 95)
74 Cumberland Ave. #2
Asheville, NC 28801

Carol Parks
(pages 75-79)
322 Westover Dr.
Asheville, NC 28801

Ken Pitts
(page 34)
c/o Frugal Farmer
95 Cherry St.
Asheville, NC 28801

Dan Reiser
(page 98)
c/o Design Lab
45 Cisco Rd.
Asheville, NC 28805

Mimi & Patty Schleicher
(page 22)
P.O. Box 1005
Weaverville, NC 28787

Larry Scholtz
(pages 52-53)
50 Glendale Ave.
Asheville, NC 28803

Jill Schwartz
(page 115)
c/o Elements
11 West 20th St.
New York, NY 10011

R. Vincent Smith
(pages 126-127)
11 Lakewood Rd.
Hendersonville, NC 28739

Allison Stern
(pages 112-113)
2325 Third St., #429
San Francisco, CA 94107

Helen Suits
(page 73)
5640 SW 57th Ave.
Gainesville, FL 32608

Ford Thomas
(page 36)
c/o Benchmarks
108 Main St.
Baton Rouge, LA 70801

Sharon Tompkins
(pages 21-22, 59-71)
Jessica Host
(page 23)
12 Caledonia Rd.
Asheville, NC 28803

Kathy Triplett
(page 99)
175 McDavis Cove Rd.
Weaverville, NC 28787

Larry Walther
(page 84)
22 Summer Circle
Clyde, NC 28721

Sue Wheeler
(pages 110-111)
c/o Sunray
405 Upper Glady Fork Rd.
Candler, NC 28715

Ellen Zahorec
(pages 2, 26-29, 74, 88,
   118-119, 123, 129,
   132-136)
1418 Country Club Rd.
Brevard, NC 28712

SUGGESTED READING

Banister, Manly. *Making Picture Frames in Wood.* NY,NY: Sterling Publishing Co., 1982.

Chappell, James. *The Potter's Complete Book of Clay & Glazes.* NY, NY: Watson-Guptil Publications, 1977.

Frank, Vivien. *An Introduction to Picture Framing.* NJ: Chartwell Books, 1990.

Innes, Jocasta. *Paint Magic.* Pantheon, 1992.

Isenberg, Anita & Seymour. *How to Work in Stained Glass.* Radnor, PA: Chilton Book Co., 1972.

Kiskalt, Isolde. *Dough Crafts.* NY, NY: Sterling/Lark Books, 1991.

McCloud, Kevin. *Decorative Style Most Original.* S & S Trade, 1990.

McGraw, Sheila. *Papier-Mâché Today.* Firefly Books, Ltd., 1990.

Newman, Thelma, Jay Hartly, Lee Scott. *The Frame Book.* NY: Crown Publishers, Inc., 1974.

O'Neil, Isabel. *Art of the Painted Finish for Furniture & Decoration.* Morrow, 1980.

Paine, Melanie. *Fabric Magic.* Pantheon, 1987.

Rhodes, Daniel. *Clay & Glazes for the Potter.* Radnor, PA: Chilton Book Co., 1973.

Shannon, Faith. *Paper Pleasures: The Creative Guide to Papercraft.* NY: Grove Press, 1987.

Stearns, Lynn. *Papermaking.* Asheville, NC: Lark Books, 1992.

Sutton, Ann. *The Structure of Weaving.* Asheville, NC: Lark Books, 1992.

Taylor, Carol. *Marbling Paper & Fabric.* NY, NY: Sterling/Lark Books, 1991.

METRIC EQUIVALENCY

Inches	CM
1/8	0.3
1/4	0.6
3/8	1.0
1/2	1.3
5/8	1.6
3/4	1.9
7/8	2.2
1	2.5
1-1/4	3.2
1-1/2	3.8
1-3/4	4.4
2	5.1
2-1/2	6.4
3	7.6
3-1/2	8.9
4	10.2
4-1/2	11.4
5	12.7
6	15.2
7	17.8
8	20.3
9	22.9
10	25.4
11	27.9
12	30.5
13	33.0
14	35.6
15	38.1
16	40.6
17	43.2
18	45.7
19	48.3
20	50.8

INDEX

A
Acid-free 14
Angle cuts 11, 39, 117
Antiquing 21, 51

B
Batik......................72, 73
Bevel cut 12, 128

C
Carving 31, 38, 50
Ceramics.............94-96, 99
Clamps......................8, 10
Copper.................106-108
Crayons ...24, 26, 135, 138

D
Découpage 51, 86, 88
Dry mounting...............14

E
Easels 16, 43, 46, 100
Experimentation.......6, 24, 50, 114

F
Feathers 117
Foam-core 14, 24, 72, 118-119, 128
Foundation 8, 19, 24, 72, 80, 114

G
Gilding..............19, 61, 62
Glass beads 55-57, 120
Glazes 59, 96
Grapevine 39, 44-49

H
Hicks frames 33, 59, 67

I
Inlay........................30, 32

L
Leather......................117
Ledge 16, 37
Liners........9, 128, 140-142

M
Marbling 22, 52, 65, 67, 86, 87, 137, 142
Mosaic 41, 42, 94, 97

N
Newspaper 25, 86, 89

O
Ovals.........12, 75, 79, 124

P
Pewter 112
Pine needles..............84-85
Plexiglass 16, 36, 108
Plywood..8, 24, 30, 39, 50, 52, 54, 56, 72

R
Rabbet..........8, 10, 37, 40, 54, 76
Reeds......................81-83

S
Safety 13, 30, 38
Soldering 100-106
Spacers ...14, 122, 137, 137
Steel 110-111
Stock mouldings....8-9, 55, 56, 120, 125

T
Table saw 8, 30, 33, 34, 56
Tin 106, 109
Tree Bark.................38, 139
Twigs 38, 41-43, 50, 55